Look Like Man
Think Like God

"WOW"... Many authors are afraid to tell the Truth...but not Mr. Jones! He has candidly exposed his past failures to the Word of God to help you live a successful life. This is a very REAL book written by a REAL guy I personally know. You are in for a special treat!

Dr. Rico D. Short
Root Canal Specialist to the Stars!
Motivational Speaker and
Author of "Getting to the Root of your Problem:
365 Days of Inspirational Thinking"

The one thing that stands out is Robert's ability to share his vulnerability and the hope that the Lord Jesus Christ is more than able to lift us up and out of every darkness into His glorious light. Congratulations, Robert, on a wonderful effort to convey truth.

Jack Valentino
Pastor of His House Church International,
Christ Community Church,
President of Sword of The Spirit Healing Ministries, Inc

Look Like Man

Think Like God

I'm Learning How and So Can You

ROBERT JONES

FIRST EDITION

ISBN: 978-1-936989-81-2

Library of Congress Control Number: 2012919585

Published by
NewBookPublishing.com, a division of Reliance Media, Inc.
515 Cooper Commerce, #140, Apopka, FL 32703
NewBookPublishing.com

Printed in the United States of America

Foreward

As the French would say, "*Le encantará esta historia:*" You will love this story. Why? In this book, Jones opens his inner chambers to give you a full appraisal, or the estimation or assessment of the values that gave him the freedom to live and to live life in full value. He is hoping as you read his ingenious insights, it might save you from a calamity he had to crawl through to find fresh air for a collapsed heart of love.

Jones uses the word *practice* in a very tractable and predictable outcome, if done consistently. It is the training, exercising, and really the drilling of the manner of living the values of Christ to improve the performance that leads to joy or pleasure instead of loss and sorrow.

The chapter titles are intriguing, fascinating:

- ***The Power of a Negative Thought***
- ***Stuck at the Gate***
- ***Satan's Tool Box***
- ***God's Wisdom Is Life's Ultimate GPS***

Robert was not a reader in his earlier life; but now he is writing a best-seller in his maturity. It is not important what a person says in the beginning of life as much as what he or she says at the end of life.

This is your advantage, then, in reading his story.

Robert says, "There was a tremendous amount of bitter seed in the form of fear and trust that was planted in my life during early childhood, through my adolescent years, and beyond. The bitter seeds became unfruitful crops that caused havoc in my life."

Then he concludes, "These crops needed to be taken to the throne of God where only He has the power to sever them at their deepest roots." And he lives to know that truth. He insightfully says, "These crippling thoughts must be dealt with from time to time. The inability to trust can be devastating in any relationship" and always leads to fear, he concludes. Robert urges his readers to harness those fears, distrust, and negative thoughts and emotions and actually use them to move our lives forward instead of backward or becoming "stuck at the gate."

Robert is a friend from the years of his confusion and crippling disorders to this day of confidence, courage, and now as an author. He practices what he teaches, and the appraisal is sound. Read his book. It will give insights that have been hidden in the dark confusion of life's crises.

I am pleased to introduce to you Robert Jones, my friend.

Dr. Don H. Polston, PhD.

Acknowledgements

I first want to thank the Lord for having his protective hand on my life long before I came to know him, and for depositing the wisdom and knowledge in me to begin and complete this book. I'm blessed because He chose me before the foundations of the world. This book is dedicated to my wonderful and amazing daughters, Sarah, Rita, and Brittany, and my handsome grandson, Brayden, who have all been an inspiration to me in walking free. To my nephew, Shannon Jones and his wife Roxanne. I appreciate your love and support over the years! I will always be grateful to you. Thank you! Special thanks to Armando Lissarrague for being obedient to the Lord in sharing Christ with me. I didn't have a clue about life and how to live it until the Lord spoke life in me through Armando. Then there's my dear Dr. Polston, who is one of the wisest men I have ever known. Dr. Polston was my first Pastor, and spoke life into me during the first ten years of my Christian life. Thank you, Dr. Polston, for all the wisdom you have poured into my life. I will always be grateful to you in more ways than you will ever know.

To my dear friend Jeff Couey, a very special thank you for leading the way for me to meet Pastor Jack Valentino of, Sword of The Spirit Healing Ministries, where my healing began. We met in the locker room at the gym where we both trained. As I was sitting on the bench, eyes closed and in deep thought, on the down side of praying he says - are you praying? I was going through a divorce at that time and he recommended that I go see Pastor Jack. Thanks to Pastor Jack for all the wisdom and the healing the Lord blessed me with because of his obedience to God as a trusted vessel in leading me through the healing process. I would also like to thank Bishop Bolin, and his son Pastor Jason for speaking life into my spirit for many years at the Church I now attend, Trinity Chapel, in Powder Springs, Georgia.

I would also like to acknowledge a few of my other close friends whom I'm in close contact with on a regular basis – Bill Flanagan, Bill Farmer, Darren Wood, Robert Lopez, and Ross Marshall - all of whom have had a part in my healing and growth process. I'm very blessed to have friends like you who love me and accept me for who I am. I want to send a very special thanks to my dear friend, Robert Lopez of 29:11 Photography, for shooting the photograph for the back cover. Thanks Bobby! I would also like to send a special thanks to my editor, Ondra Krouse Dismukes, Phd in English, and an instructor in American Literature and English Composition. I'm very grateful for your expertise and generosity. Also, thanks to all of the people of whom I have been in relationship with throughout the many years of my life – because without those experiences, good or bad, this book would have never came to be.

Table of Contents

Chapter One ......The Power of a Negative Thought 9

Chapter Two ......Stuck at the Gate 25

Chapter Three....The Clock is Ticking 43

Chapter Four .....The Dark Road: "Satan's Tool Box" 53

Chapter Five......Get Bitter or Better: The Choice is Yours 69

Chapter Six........Change Your Perspective; Change Your Life....... 83

Chapter Seven ...God Wants To Do a New Thing in You............... 95

Chapter Eight ....Eight Deadly Sins
                    That Leave No Room for God 107

Chapter Nine .....God's Wisdom is Life's Ultimate GPS 127

Chapter Ten ....Running the Race 149

Why I Wrote This Book 167

Author Bio 169

Chapter One

The Power of a Negative Thought

Mark Twain said the man who doesn't read good books has no advantage over the man who can't read them. That's an astounding statement and is so true. During my early years, I was not one to pick up a book to read because I just didn't like to read, and now I'm writing one; amazing, isn't it? After reading this first chapter, you will come to know that it was only because of the divine appointment of the Lord that I was able to write this book. This chapter is a short synopsis of some of the things that I went through early in life. There was a tremendous amount of bitter seed in the form of fear and trust that was planted in my life during my early childhood years, through my adolescent years, and beyond. The bitter seeds became unfruitful crops that caused havoc in my life. These crops needed to be taken to the throne of God, where only He has the power to sever them at their deepest roots.

One day I hope to share these and other nuggets of truth with men and women, young and old, all over the world. My hope and prayer is that all who reads this book will have a greater understanding of how their past, present, and future thinking, thoughts, habits, and attitudes can affect their lives, and to help guide them to a more productive way of thinking and living by the renewing of their minds, therefore enhancing their lives and the lives of others around them. I hope and pray that this book touches the lives of all "young and old" all over the world.

Most people, if not all, have had the negative thoughts of fear and trust at some point in their lives and may continue to have those crippling thoughts from time to time. The inability to trust can be devastating in any relationship, and trust issues are typically, if not always, connected to fear in some form or fashion. Fear, in my opinion, is the most negative and hindering thought anyone could ever have, because when we fear it opens the door for the enemy to trick you into other crippling thoughts. When these feelings of fear and worry become thoughts, they can and will become powerful adversaries in your life if you don't know how to harness them and use them to your advantage. Yes it's easy to say don't fear because the Lord tells us to fear not. Why did he tell us that? Of course! He told us to fear not because he doesn't want us to fear.

The Lord also told us to fear not because he knew the enemy was going to try to tempt us with fear. So, it's not a matter of will you fear again; it's more of a matter of when fear tries to rear its ugly head in your life, will you be ready? What will you do? How will you react? Will you know how to harness it to your advantage? There are many books out there on the subject of trials and tribulations, and everything else under the sun. I don't have the answers, but I know the one who has all the answers and holds the truth to all things. It's Christ and Christ alone. Jesus Christ is the answer, has always been the answer, and always will be the answer - PERIOD! There is no deliverance from anything apart from Christ. The majority of material contained in this book came from my life's experiences and the things that I've learned from them, along with some helpful thoughts from the Pastors to whom I have had the privilege of listening to over the past thirty years. God bless you all.

I don't have all the answers; but I personally know the one who does. His name is Jesus!

One of the things I want to talk about in this chapter is how to harness these negative emotions, attitudes, and perspectives that are brought on by fear and actually use them to help us move forward in life. When negative feelings and emotions come, and they will, let's use them for our purposes instead of letting them use us for their purposes. Fear in and of itself is not the factor that hurts us; it's what we do with the fear and, more importantly, what we let it do to us that can harm us. Someone once said that only 10% of life is what happens to us and 90% of life is how we react to it. There's much truth to this statement. Our reactions to circumstances and life in general set the tone of our day; and that tone, whether positive or negative, has a tendency to carry into the next day, next week, and beyond. When our inner spirit feels threatened, we fear. When our spirit is at ease and not threatened, we feel love - we feel safe.

I'd like to share a personal testimony with you how my spirit was threatened early in life by fear and then share how the Lord gave me the power to overcome the darkness that tried to overtake me later in life. It would be silly for me to say that I hope no one else has ever experienced what I experienced in Junior High School because I surely can't be the only one that has ever experienced these things. But I would like to say that my heart goes out to those of you who have experienced similar trials. I truly hope those of you who can relate to this text will benefit from this chapter, as well as the entire book. My testimony begins at the end of my last year of elementary school, which was 6th grade. My grades were mostly E's and S's which are equivalent to A's and B's; so, during those years, I was doing very well in school. I loved school back then and enjoyed everything that had to do with that experience. I quickly learned that Junior High School was a whole different ball game.

The Junior High School that I attended was not short on bullies, and I'm thinking they all followed me there. Here I am walking down the hall minding my own business and these two football players, who looked like giants, push me, one from each side knocking me to the floor for no reason. I would also get cornered in the restrooms, hallways, and any other place these bullies were, and I would often get asked, "Do you consider yourself black or white?" Before I had a chance to respond, they would answer, "You look black to me." Almost every day, three or four boys, much bigger than I, would corner me, threaten me, and push me around. Yes, I told my parents; and my parents did complain to the principal, but nothing was ever done to alleviate the situation.

Now that may not sound like much to you; but, in seventh grade, I was a super feather and, these boys were football players at least six inches taller than I. Needless to say, I was intimidated. Here's a good one for you. Swimming class was every Tuesday, and we were forced to swim naked. Why? I don't know and no one ever had explained that nonsense. That was one of the most humiliating experiences ever. In today's society, that surely would not be allowed. Back in those days, we were disciplined with swats; and in swimming class, when it was time for someone to get disciplined with a swat, the coach would walk the less fortunate one to the end of the diving board and tell him to grab his ankles. He would then give him a hard swat on the bare butt with a huge wooden paddle, and the boy, needless to say, would fall into the pool. Whenever I saw that, it would scare the tar out of me, mostly because I didn't know how to swim. At that point, I learned how to tread water very quickly, but I never learned how to swim at that time because I made it a point to skip that class every week. Eventually, though, I learned how to swim in college.

I was determined to find a way to get myself out of school, or should I say free from the abuse that I received when I was there. At that point in my life, I saw no reason whatsoever to attend school, and I was willing to do whatever necessary to rid myself of the situation. I had to come up with a plan and very quickly, I might add. Midway through my first year of Junior High School, I began riding my bike to school; and every day, I went on an extended ride and never made it to school. After several weeks I was found out, and my mom decided to start driving me to school. After my mom dropped me off, I would walk in the front door, head directly out the back door, and go for a long walk home. Yes, my parents disciplined me; but, at the same time, they loved me, were there for me, and were sorry for what I'd been going through. My parents knew everything that was going on.

I then started to put up a fuss about going to school, so my mom would often call the school cop to come and get me and take me to school. So, here I am in familiar territory again. I had to come up with another plan to escape the harassment and embarrassment that I received while in school. So here's my new idea: I would show up in Home Room; and, after the first period, I would walk out the door and head for home. I did this in the coldest parts of the winter too, in Iowa. I recall times when my feet got so wet and cold, I would find a place to sit and take off my shoes and socks. Believe it or not my feet felt warmer when barefoot and out in the elements as compared to being in my wet shoes and socks. Talk about the school of hard knocks – I know and attended that school very well for quite some time. At the end of the school year, I had missed approximately 60 days of school. I received all F's and U's. I hated that place, and I never wanted to go back. When school ended, I was a happy camper. The following year, they passed me on to the 8th grade, and I never understood why, because I failed every subject I was enrolled in. The same harassment continued during the eighth grade; in fact, it got worse. I think my school got first draft pick on the best and biggest bullies that year.

The football players were bigger and meaner, and we were still swimming naked. So, here I am, finding myself in that familiar place again, having to come up with another plan to skip class. I had the same routine as in the beginning: of walking through the front door and out the back door; but one day I got caught as I was leaving, and I never did that again. Here's my new plan. I would show up in Home Room; and, after the 2nd period and sometimes the 3rd period, I would start my long walk home. It took them much longer to catch on to me this way. I missed 90-plus days in the eighth grade and received straight F's. I dropped out of school, after failing the seventh and eighth grades, with basically a 6th-grade education. I let the negative thoughts of fear and intimidation steal one of the most precious parts of my life. Those times are gone forever, and I can never get them back. This is why it's so important to know what to do with fear when it comes, because our lives and precious memories are much too valuable to waste. I had enough fearful and negative thoughts in seventh and eighth grade for several lifetimes. I was just a kid at the time, and handling those kinds of issues in a positive manner when you're thirteen and fourteen years of age is not a walk in the park, especially if there wasn't an example to follow. I didn't know the

Lord then, but it's obvious to me now that His protecting hand was upon my life.

I quit school when I was fifteen and later on, around the age of seventeen I began my Rock N Roll phase as a Rock drummer and went through the partying stage, and experimenting with drugs and pot. I did that for several years; and was delivered and healed from all that nonsense shortly after I came to know the Lord. I started working full-time in the family asphalt construction business and did so until somewhere around the age of twenty-two. If I had to do it all over again, I would surely finish high school and attend a good baseball college. I loved baseball with a passion; and, if I'd had someone to tell me that I could, I would have pursued baseball. It humbles me to think what I could have accomplished if I'd had guidance and direction. I left home when I was about twenty two and headed for New York City – Yeah, right! I didn't have a clue; but I left anyway and lived there for about four months. Although, I never intended on being a model, I ended up going to a modeling school because they told me they had an acting program, as well, and my intended purpose for going to New York was to study acting. I had no guidance or direction in my life until the age of twenty-four, and I must admit that I have thought about how different my life would be if I'd had someone to help guide me.

I did graduate from modeling school and also was coached by the casting director of the soap opera *As the World Turns*. Her name was Joan Anderson and I'll never forget her. She said there was a place for me there; but I was completely out of my comfort zone in New York City, and I soon headed for home. That place scared the tar out of me, too. Here, again, fear set in, and I chose to run. I hadn't learned yet how to cope when out of my comfort zone. Little did I know, then, that I could have learned how to be comfortable in unfamiliar surroundings. I often wonder what would have transpired if I had stayed there. When I arrived home in Iowa, I was hired to work at a real estate company, and that's where I got saved and came to know the Lord. I then enrolled in real estate school to prepare for the state exam to get my real estate license. I passed the exam, but only after taking the test five times. Well, what else would you expect with a 6th-grade education? Brad, my real estate instructor, said that he couldn't believe how I stayed with it. He said I was relentless and just wouldn't give up. I now know that it was only because of the Lord that I was able to keep going and pass the test. After passing the exam, I went to work at the real estate company where I was hired. Praise the Lord! This is where I met Armando. Armando was my boss.

One afternoon, he asked me to come into his office because he wanted to talk with me about something. He started talking about God, Jesus Christ, being born again, and being saved. At first I truly thought this guy was off his rocker. I remember thinking to myself, "saved from what? – I'm a good person; and I'm Catholic, for crying out loud!" That was the winter of 1978 when I accepted the Lord as my personal Savior. Thanks, Armando, for being obedient to the Lord and showing me the way. I will never forget you, my friend. This book is partially created out of Armando's obedience to the Lord. Armando had Bible study with me once a week for nearly a year, and that's what it's all about, now isn't it – bringing people to know the Lord and disciplining them? I soon learned that selling real estate wasn't for me. At that time of my life, I was going through some trying times about my future. The Lord put it in my spirit to go back to school. I enrolled in a junior college – Hawkeye Institute of Technology. I had to learn everything I missed out on in the seventh and eighth grades, and high school, as well to prepare me to pass all the exams. Having to learn so much in so little time was not an easy task; but, praise the Lord, I got it done! During my course work, I was asked to give the commencement speech at graduation. That was one of the coolest things I've ever done. After graduation, I went on to attend the University of Northern Iowa, which was a challenge, as well, and was somewhat overwhelming, to say the least. I remember, in General Chemistry 1, when I first heard the phrase "Avogadro's number," and then I saw the number 6.02 x 10 to the 23rd power. I immediately felt fear because I had never heard of Avogadro's number, let alone the numerals that represent it. My thinking was, I'm way out of my element here; and I was. I had no idea what a periodic table was and had never even seen one before. So, here I am sitting in class with a hundred teenagers who are fresh out of high school and are familiar with all that's going on; and I, on the other hand, have the look of a deer in headlights, to say the least. I didn't have a clue!

Did fear set in? Was I uncomfortable and threatened? Did I want to leave immediately? The answers are yes, yes, and yes. I didn't leave or drop the class but I didn't pass it either. Next semester, I took it again. I understood the class a little more this time around, but not enough to pass it. I was going to pass that class if it was the last thing I ever did! My pride was at stake this time around. The very moment I saw my grade the second time around, God instilled something inside me that said, "Don't run, and don't quit." The Lord knew just what was going on in my mind, like running, defeat, protective walls going up, and everything else. Fear tried to overtake me; but, praise the Lord, He that lives in me is greater than he that lives in the world and also greater than the fear that tried to overtake me.

"When threatened, don't run.
Stay the course and confront it with the Word"
Like Joyce Meyer says – "Do it afraid!"
I've been learning to do it afraid for thirty-three years.

The Lord told me to embrace fear and not run as I did in middle school. Granted, this was a different kind of fear than my experience in junior high school; but, nevertheless, it's fear. Embracing fear is being able to get out of your comfort zone, do the thing that you're afraid of, and stand up for what you believe in when facing fear. Be a man and woman of God, and stand up to what you're afraid of and believe in. It may be something that you need to do; and, at the present time, you just don't have the courage to do it, so you just live in the status quo. Men and women of faith lean upon Christ. As children of God, we need to understand where the real power comes from and in whom it resides. If you use fear in a positive fashion, it can and will activate the power that has already been instilled in you, by God and the word of God, and propel you forward and closer to the will of God and His intended purpose for your life.

The enemy might have won a few battles in my middle school years, but I won the war later on. I did go on to complete three years, successfully, at the University of Northern Iowa. I did not graduate due to a combination of my, then, wife losing her job, my father's illness, and my having to take over the family asphalt construction business. Do the negative thoughts of fear still try to creep in? Of course they do. If you're human and breathing, I guarantee that those negative thoughts of fear will try to come in from time to time. The best way to defeat fear is to embrace it. Embracing fear does not mean that we like it. Embracing fear is the opposite of running from it. We must hit it head on with the power of the Holy Spirit through

Christ Jesus, the word of God, faith, and prayer. We must admit all our fears to God and trust him to walk with us through them. Some of you may be thinking the Lord knows perfectly well that we have fears and he knows exactly what those fears are; so why do we have to confess them to him? Here's why: Because when we share our fears and everything else with the Lord, we are asking him to join us in them. We are leaning on him and trusting him to walk with us through all of them. We are, in essence, asking him to keep his hand on all of those areas that trouble and taunt us. This is exactly what the Lord wants. Don't you want the Lord to keep his loving hand on all of your circumstances, trials, tribulations, and fears? Of course you do, and the best way to do that is to include him, verbally, in all things through prayer. It's no different than communicating with your spouse, girlfriend, or friend. If we want or need help from them, we must first invite them to do so by asking. I'm not quite sure who coined the "Do it afraid" phrase, but Joyce Meyer is the first person that I heard use it.

That's a good phrase, and I like what John Wayne said as well – "Courage is being scared to death and saddling up anyway." In all reality, I think many, if not most, of us have been doing it afraid and saddling up in spite of our fears for many years. I've been doing it afraid and saddling up for thirty-three years now, and you know what I have found out? All of the things that I was afraid of have never harmed me because they never happened. I'm sure that you have experienced many of the same fears that most of us have experienced at some point in time. We live in an evil and wicked world; and, because we live in an evil and wicked world, evil and wicked things are going to happen. These bad things don't just happen to bad or good people, they happen to all people. That being said, without Christ in our lives, evil is stronger than we are; but, because we are born again believers and are indwelt with the Holy Spirit, we have power over evil forces. When fear and negative thoughts try to creep in; use them to your advantage. Let them propel you through by drawing you closer to the Lord and His word. There are two scriptures that I clung to during those tough times in college and still do today, and they are 1 John 4:4: "He that lives in me is greater than he that lives in the world," and, Philippians 4:13: "I can do all things through Christ who strengthens me." When we fight back with scripture, we're inviting the living God in Jesus Christ to take part in the circumstances of our lives. The Lord will be with us every step of the way as he walks with us through everything with which we're faced in this life. There is nothing on this planet that we can't get through when we tap into the power of God. The power of the Lord rests in His word, but we must have faith and believe. The words in the Bible are not just words manipulated by men and printed on pages and put in a book called the Bible. The Bible is God's love letter to the human race. There is no greater and more powerful force in your possession than the word of God and prayer.

"If we want the Lord to help us through our circumstances, we must ask Him to be part of our circumstances."

Fear is one of two things: It's an emotion caused by some stimulus that has had some kind of an impact in your life, or it's a new stimulus that you have never experienced before. Either way, fear is an emotion caused by some kind of stimulus. For example, there's emotional fear; and when emotional fear comes into play, it's typically, but not always, tied to a relationship issue that was not pleasant in your past. I'd like to use this analogy to share this thought.

When a circumstance comes about in an existing relationship that brings back memories from a past relationship, and its effects were devastating, we are pre-conditioned to fear in the present relationship because we think we're going to have the same result as in the past relationship. Fear can also be a healthy thing in terms of it helping us recognize things that can harm us. Whether the fear is protecting us from a relationship issue or protecting us from something physical such as skydiving, swimming in the ocean, or mountain climbing, fear does have some protecting qualities. I'm not suggesting that we should be afraid of these things. I am using them as examples only. These types of fears can be termed respectful fear. Fear is a very personal issue, and everyone expresses fear in different ways. Some people deal with their fear in a passive manner and do nothing because of pride and other factors, and others deal with fear in a more exaggerated fashion, and sometimes that individual exhibits radical behaviors to deal with it. Then there are others who deal with their fear in a more logical fashion, like admitting that their afraid and what they're afraid of and taking a proactive role in doing something about it, through faith, prayer and the word of God. In my opinion, this is the best way to deal with fear. "TAKE IT TO GOD"

How we deal with fear is important and identifying the things that trigger fear is equally important. Fear when used properly can produce meaningful and positive results, but it's not required or the preferred way to produce meaningful and positive results. I'm not saying that fear is good because the Lord tells us to fear not, but I am suggesting that when it comes – learn how to use it to your advantage. All I'm suggesting here is when fear comes use it, don't run and fret, hit it head on with the word of God and Prayer. If the positive result from fear is to draw you into a closer relationship with the Lord and total dependence on him, than fear produced a meaningful and positive result into your life. I believe the Lord may allow certain things to happen in our lives to bring us to a place of total dependence on Him. This has been true many times throughout my Christian life.

"If you have fears, confess them to the Lord."

It's common knowledge that your mind can hold only one thought at a time; and, if that thought is negative in nature, typically, a fearful response will occur. All habits are learned behavior and become habitual by means of repeated occurrences of that behavior. Have you ever wondered why evil habits and thoughts are always available to us in any amount, and why good wholesome thoughts and habits elude us? It's because we live in a sinful world; and, in a sinful world, these are the kinds of things we must deal with every day of our lives. We must re-program and pre-program our minds with the word of God in order to overcome the wickedness of the world's patterns.

The scripture passage that comes to mind is Romans 12:2, which says; "Do not conform any longer to the patterns of this world, but be transformed by the renewing of your mind. Then you will be able to attest and approve what God's will is, his good pleasing, and perfect will." When we know God's good, pleasing, and perfect will, it's easier to fear not. It's also easier to fear not when you're praising the Lord. The power of the Lord is released in our circumstances when we praise Him through them. I read a book about twenty-five years ago titled, *Power in Praise*. I'm not sure if it's still in print; but, if you can find it, I highly recommend buying it and reading it until the words move from your head to your heart.

Final Thoughts

The Lord told us to fear not because he knew long before we were created that we would fear. The Lord also knew that when fear came, if we didn't deal with it in a positive way through his word, faith, and prayer, that it would get the best of us. Fear in and of itself is not what harms us, but what can and will harm us is what we allow fear to do in us and through us. How we respond to fear is what determines the outcome. If we come against the negativity that comes from fear immediately with the word of God, that's the beginning of overcoming fear. The key word, here, is *immediately*; don't let it linger. We must apply the word of God immediately instead of letting whatever it is fester for hours, days, and weeks-on-end. That's why the Bible tells us to meditate on scripture – memorize it so you have it at the tip of your tongue at all times. When our minds are renewed by the word of God, we see things from the Lord's perspective. When we are able to identify our fears in terms of what we are afraid of and why, they can then be harnessed in such a way that we can use them to benefit ourselves instead of harming ourselves. When fear comes, and it may come again, use it to your advantage and let it draw you closer to the Lord in prayer and study time in the Word. Bathe yourself in the word of God and prayer, and fear will flee. When we know the will of God and praise him, even though we are fearful of something, the fear will eventually subside, because when we're confident of the Lord's will, and while praising him, it's difficult to focus on the negative. We must know that there's power in praising and worshiping the Lord Jesus Christ.

Chapter Two

Stuck at the Gate

I board the plane at Reagan Airport in Virginia, on my way back to Atlanta. After all the passengers take their seats and the door is shut and locked we are ready to taxi out, the pilot announces that all flights to Atlanta are grounded by the FAA due to stormy weather conditions. We were stuck at the gate. It was about noon. As I was sitting in the plane on the tarmac, I decided to make a call to a friend in Atlanta to see what was going on, and he said the wind is blowing a reported fifty miles per hour, and it was as dark as night at noon day. Many people are stuck at life's gate and can't seem to get off the ground and soar because there's always some kind of storm going on in their lives. Sound familiar? Do you know someone like that? I surely do, and that someone was me. I know beyond a shadow of a doubt that I was the cause of the majority of the storms in my life, and it was because I was straddling the fence as a Christian. When we become children of God we are accountable to the Lord in all we do. I knew exactly what I was doing and I knew better, and that's why I was stuck at the gate of living life more abundantly. I was reaping exactly what I had sown. I thought I could look at pornography, hold on to anger, and fear, and stray away from reading the Bible and praying to the Father, and everything would be ok. I thought just because I asked for forgiveness everything would be peachy. There were times when the urge was so strong to look at pornography, I would rationalize and say just one more time than I'll stop. I didn't completely stop but stayed away for several months at a time, then when I felt better about myself, I would go right back to doing it again. I felt like I hated myself and became angry within. Yes the Lord forgave me every time, but I failed to see for a very long time that the consequences had to be paid for my lack of obedience to the Lord and His word. Are you stuck at life's gate? And if so, what's got you stuck? Many times, over the course of our lives, difficult circumstances come into our lives, regardless of who we are. And when they come, sometimes they have a tendency to come without any notice. When I say problems come without notice, I'm not saying that they came suddenly, because most problems just don't arrive in our lives that way. Most problems started in incubation way back when and we either ignored the signs or were not aware of the signs. Most of us choose to ignore the signs of problems, and that's exactly what I did.

"Have you ever felt like you were stuck at the gate of life?"

Most of us have been in weather-related stormy conditions before, and have seen the results of damaging winds; and I'm sure that you'll agree: it's not a pleasant experience. The storms of life can be just as damaging and uncomfortable. Have you ever felt like you're being tossed to and fro and running, uphill, against the wind? Are you stuck at life's gate? Is the wind blowing so hard that you can't get on the runway of life because it's too scary, dark, cloudy, or windy? Sometimes life's problems can get out of control and overbearing, but they don't have to prevent you from moving toward a more productive life. Typically, the most successful people in life are not smarter than the average person. Successful people have the attitude that if there's a wall, there's a way. I'm borrowing that line from my dear Pastor, Dr. Don Polston's book, titled *If There's a Wall There's a Way*. When you get a few minutes, check out his website: donhpolston.com. There, you will find the book *Where There's a Wall There's a Way* and may other books that we all need to read. He was my first Pastor when I got saved in 1979, and I must say that he is one of the wisest men I have ever met. Thank you, Dr. Polston, for your leadership all those years, and for being a true man of God.

Successful people have the attitude that no matter what's going on in their lives, they will find a way to go around, over, or through whatever kind of storm is facing them. To go around, over, or through the storm, we must, first, identify the kind of storm we're facing. There are storms that keep you in the dark, and there are storms that are so intense that you can barely think about anything else but the storm. Several times in the course of our lives, we go through personal storms of various kinds. Are you ready for the runway? Brace yourself, because you may be taking off sooner than you think.

"Identify the storm; then, attack it."

Identifying the types of storms in our lives is crucial because we must know what we're up against so we can make a plan of attack. Identifying the type of storm is not always easy because most of us aren't willing to be exposed. Exposing ourselves is necessary in identifying exactly where that nagging thing came from that has been troubling us for years. Most of us aren't trained in identifying the source of our pain; and, when this is the case, a professional should be considered to help identify that source and bring it to the throne of God in Christ Jesus in prayer. I want to emphasize that the kind of professional I'm talking about is a Christian who is trained in the healing ministries of the Lord. Not all councilors are trained and have the gift of identifying the sources of our pain. We'll talk more about this later.

"The attitude of your thoughts always remains positive, and faith and action must be tied to it."

After identifying the storm, the first thing I do to attack is pray and seek the Lord's wisdom and guidance. I pray about everything and include God in all decision-making. Have I always done this? Regrettably, not! One of the things I now like to do is verbally give the Lord permission to break, conquer, and overcome my will. I'll be the first to admit: I've stepped ahead of God's time table and walked right out of his will and have given in to my flesh more than once and have paid dearly for it. One of the most important questions that I never asked myself in the past is; "Did I cause the storm?"

After seeking the Lord's council through prayer and the reading of His word, along with the council from a mentor who truly walks with the Lord, I carefully examine the circumstances to see if there's any evidence of my storm being self-inflicted. If the evidence points the cause to me, I ask myself one question and I'll share that one question with you later in this chapter.

If I'm not the cause of the storm, I examine the situation to see how I might have been helping the storm along. Granted, everyone on the planet has gone through, or will go through, different kinds of storms in their lives that are no fault of his/her own. Life happens to everyone and will continue to happen. I make this statement in defense of the many wonderful people whom I have had the pleasure and honor to meet, and to the great people whom I will never get a chance to meet in my life: people who have been through some trying times with no fault of their own. I would also like to point out that even if you're not the cause of your storm, there's a possibility that you could be helping the storm along and giving it power over your situation because your behavior and your thinking are at odds with the Lord and His word.

There was a time in my life when I couldn't figure out why I was going through certain struggles, let alone attempting to get through them successfully. I have come to the conclusion that the Lord let the storm winds blow in my life to get me to a place where He wanted me to be and positioned me so that He could work with me and mold me and shape me into the person that He wants me to be. I now believe that I was of no use to the Lord the way I was. Please don't mistake this comment for being of no value to the Lord. Everyone has value to the Lord, but not everyone allows the Lord to use them the way He wants. The Lord used the storms of life to mold and shape me so He could get me to do what He wanted me to do. If we keep ignoring the signs, we are like children on a merry go round: thinking we're going somewhere but not. I would never have arrived to the place of change if it wasn't for the storms that the Lord let come into my life. The Lord says it this way in Psalm 119:71 "It was good for me to be afflicted so that I might learn your decrees." This caused me to think that I should always look for the new possibilities in the storm and also look for the Lord in the storm. I guarantee that if you're paying enough attention and seeking God, you will find the Lord in the center of most, if not all, of your storms; and, in the midst of it all, there will be a message and some direction there for you, as well. I also believe that if you're not spending consistent quality time in the word and prayer, you more than likely will miss the direction from the Lord. God always wants to do something new for you, in you, and through you. He will consistently take you to unfamiliar territory so he can change you and use you as a vessel for something he created you to do or be. In this process, we must always be on the lookout for the enemy because he always will try to keep us side-tracked with unfruitful circumstances, activities, and friendships.

Much of the time, both for single men and women, it's an unhealthy relationship with the opposite sex. The bottom line, here, is that when the Lord tries to direct us in the storms of life, and also when everything in life seems peachy, we must not take detours. As I look back on my life, I took more detours with my decisions and choices that were out of the will of God and, in the process, postponed the Lord's plan for me. I made it through, but only by the grace of God and the guidance of the Holy Spirit and the word of God. There were a few great men of God who gave me some wise council, as well. They made a few key suggestions and left it up to me to be obedient to the Lord. They always pointed me to the Lord Jesus, as well. Christ is the answer, has always been the answer, and always will be the answer. There are no substitutes for the power, love, mercy, and wisdom of God, and it only comes by way of the Holy Spirit and the word of God, which you will find in the Bible. That's the Spirit of God living in everyone who believes in the death, burial, and resurrection of Christ and believes that Christ is who he says he is. This does not vary, there are no substitutes, and there is no other way...PERIOD! This is my main reason for writing this book – pointing you toward Jesus!

If there are some of you reading this book and having a difference of opinion and belief system, hopefully my story will help give you a clearer understanding of the Christian faith. I always like to use the following analogy when I'm talking about God and His infinite wisdom of life: If someone created a software program, who's going to know more about that program than its creator? The answer is, "No one," right? The same applies to life, and you may see this next statement again because it applies to so much. Who knows more about life and the best way to live life than the one who created life?

No one! God created all of life, which means he created you. He knows everything about you and is fully aware of everything that is going on in your life, and is very capable and willing to get you through whatever it is that you're going through. For the longest time, I was keeping the storms going in my life by ignoring the truth in God's word and straddling the fence. I ignored all the signs of the things that caused the storms in my life as well. Even though I knew what was right, I did what was wrong. Sound familiar? Apostle Paul says it this way in Romans 7:15 "I do not understand what I do. For what I want to do I do not do, but what I hate I do – verse 17 "As it is, it is no longer I myself who do it, but it is sin living in me. I was keeping the storms going in my life by listening to and obeying my flesh. It's this kind of thinking that will stop you in every endeavor of life. Obedience to the word of God is the key that turns the ignition of life: the key that unlocks your next miracle, the force that stops the stormy winds, and the power to remove the blocks that are preventing you from moving forward. It's not merely reading the Word, but obedience to the Word that unleashes the power of God in our lives so we can produce what He wants us to produce and be who and what He created us to be.

"Who knows more about life than the creator of life?"

I was keeping the storms going in my life but not because of ignorance. I knew the truth, I knew the right way to live, behave, act, and think. Yes, most of the time I did what was right in the eyes of the Lord, but obedience most of the time is not what pleases the Lord. Many of my problems were arising from unwise decisions; and unwise decisions are typically bred from unwise thinking. I made decisions, alright, but the decisions were to listen to my flesh and not the Lord's voice and the prompting of the Holy Spirit, through His word and the godly council that the Lord set before me.

It's vital to please the Lord in all aspects of life because, with obedience in doing the right thing comes peace; and, when your life is peaceful, you can achieve so much more. A peaceful spirit thinks, talks, acts, and believes in an entirely different fashion than a spirit that is not at peace. Here's an analogy I like to use: You're driving and pass by a cop who has his radar gun pointing right at you. You immediately look at your speedometer and notice that you were going 20 miles over the speed limit, and then you see the bright flashing lights in your mirror. Do you remember how quickly your countenance went from a peaceful state to a somewhat nervous state? If you're at odds with the law, you're not going to be very comfortable, "at peace," when they start coming after you. Life is very similar in that when we live life in such a way that is not pleasing to the Lord, especially when we know it, it's impossible to have a peaceful spirit because our spirit is at odds with the Lord. Even if you don't feel at odds with the Lord, if you're not living in accordance with the word of God, and especially if you're not a born-again believer, you're at odds with God, whether you believe it or not. Just because you don't believe it doesn't make this fact untrue. It's impossible to receive all that God has for us if we're at odds with him. When we're at odds with the Lord and wanting to live life our way, we are, in essence, saying – BACK OFF, GOD; I GOT IT! I KNOW WHAT I'M DOING!

"Change may say you need to start thinking differently."

After much heartache and turmoil in my own life, I have come to the conclusion that most people will do something about their situation when the pain that they're going through is greater than the pain to change or to leave their situation. Then, there are those who will never change, no matter how bad life gets. Lastly, there are those who have had their share of ups and downs, but have lived a life of making choices and decisions without being at odds with the Lord. Which one are you? If what you've been doing, and the way you've been living and thinking haven't produced the results that you're looking for, do you think it might be time to take a serious look at something else and change some things? It could be your thinking, your lifestyle, your thoughts, your vocabulary, or all of the above that needs a change. I'm sure you get the idea, so I won't belabor the point.

Year after year, most of us keep doing the same things over and over and expecting different results. We're like kids on a merry-go-round thinking we're going somewhere but not. I think it's time for us to grow up and admit our shortcomings and admit that we don't have it all together like we want others to think. I'm not saying that we have to say to the world, "Hey, I'm messed up," but we must admit our shortcomings to ourselves and God, and take them to Him in prayer and ask Him to heal us of them. Then and only then can we begin the process of healing and working toward God's intended purpose for our lives. We need to change, stop playing church, and be the people that God called us to be.

"It's time to stop playing church."

I was born and raised in Iowa and have been around planting for many years; and, since I have a small bit of knowledge about farming, we're going to discuss farming and the planting of seeds of a different kind. As the scripture says in Galatians 6:7, "Do not be deceived, God cannot be mocked, a man reaps what he sows" We all will reap the fruit of our behavior, thinking, vocabulary, habits, etc.

I would like to quote Dr. Polston from one of his messages, titled "The Seed & the Sower," from many years ago, and it goes like this. "The whole kingdom of God is based on the seed principal. Everything you say, do, think, and pray, has a seed within itself that will produce precisely what you said, did, thought, or prayed." No, you're not going to win the lottery if you think and pray about it long and hard enough; and just saying positive things doesn't mean positive things are going to happen. Positive affirmation must have a catalyst to make the seed grow. The catalyst I'm talking about is putting forth effort and action with your speech and belief system. In other words, action shows faith, and it's faith that takes root and grows the seed. If you want the seed to grow, there must be faith as the catalyst. Yes, continue to speak positive words of affirmation, but make sure you apply the catalyst of action to stimulate growth from faith. We must prove that we believe what we believe by the way we act and talk.

**"Everything you say, do, think, and pray,
has a seed within itself that will produce precisely
what you said, did, thought, or prayed."**

There must be a change in your thinking and behavior for a

change to take place. There must be action tied to your belief. Just like writing this book. I could have all the experiences in the world, and keep a journal of these experiences for years, but until I started to write, and write consistently, string sentences together, structuring paragraphs, there was not going to be a complete manuscript. In order to create the best and most fulfilling lives for ourselves, we must keep the train on the tracks, and the best way to do that is to be disciplined enough to bathe ourselves in scripture, prayer, good and positive thoughts, along with faith and the all-important ingredient of action. Granted, there are some things in life over which we have no control; however, I believe we can do something about the self-inflicted storms that come into our lives. Many times, but not always, our lack of breakthroughs is due to the lack of positive affirmation from scripture, prayer, faith, and the action needed to create that new and better life for ourselves. You must do something. In my experience, the best place to start is on your knees, faced-down, and in the word of God. There are no substitutes.

"We all have our own self-inflicted wounds."

Okay; I'm not going to pull any punches here. This may be uncomfortable for some, so I'm going to talk about my experiences with wounds and life's storms of the I-caused-them kind. Before I came to know the Lord Jesus as my personal savior, if you asked me if I believed in God, I would have said "yes," with a powerful emphasis. I was not brought up in a Christian home but was always taught that there was a God and to believe in Him, and to believe that Christ died for my sins, but was never really taught how to have a personal relationship with Him and had never heard of being saved or born again until I was around twenty two years of age.

Everyone in my immediate family and including all my relatives from every corner of the country have always had a strong belief that there is a God, and had always thought that through superstitions and family traditions and other handed down family practices, that they knew who God was and was pleasing Him because of holding tight to those traditions. I say this with all due respect to my family and relatives all over the country, little did they know that none of their religious practices did and never will be pleasing to the Lord, except the faith and trust that they have in Jesus Christ apart from all their family traditions. This is what I grew up with. As with my parents, I can only teach my kids what I know and not any more. This is why it's so vital that we learn the truth about God and who he truly is from the scriptures so we can teach our children about God before someone else influences them with some form of religion that is contradictory to the word of God that doesn't glorify Christ. There's much more on this topic in the "Dark Road" chapter. This all changed for me when I got saved.

As I mentioned earlier, Armando took the time to have Bible study with me for nearly a year and this changed my life forever as I knew it. I began to start looking at my life in a whole new light and everything else around me as well. This made me start to think about the things that I was taught as growing up in light of the things that I learned on my own; that was revealed to me by the Holy Spirit. Wow, what a wake-up call that was. I will never forget that process and will always be grateful to Armando for that. Even after studying the scriptures and learning much about life and the way it should be lived, you couldn't convince me that I had anything to do with the circumstances and storms that came into my life. It was never my fault. It was always someone or something else – NOT ME! Have you ever known anyone that always had to be right and no matter what the subject was, they had all the correct answers? Have you ever known someone who always had something to say about everything and everyone, and they know everything about everything? For some reason they feel the need to give their opinion on everyone and everything, and it's not in their vocabulary to say, I just don't know, or say nothing at all. This all comes from fear, low self esteem, and the need to validate oneself. I was one of those people who had to be right and had all the answers – so I thought. Did it hurt me? Yes it did. Sometimes we create the drama in our own lives because we never want to be corrected, listen to others, seek council of the Biblical kind, and the list goes on. The Bible tells us in Proverbs 15:32 that "He who ignores discipline despises himself, but whoever heeds correction gains understanding." Please let's don't be ignorant, let's turn to God's word for guidance, and for your own good please find a good Christian friend who's walking with the Lord and plugged into the word of God to share things with from time to time. This will benefit you more than you may realize.

There are a few other scriptures that I would like to share, and the first one is Proverbs 16:18 that says, "pride goes before destruction, and a haughty spirit before stumbling", and the second one is in Isaiah 5:21 that says, "woe to those who are wise in their own eyes and clever in their own sight". Earlier in the chapter I said that I would share the one question that I asked myself if the evidence pointed toward me for causing the storm in my life. The question is… have I been prideful in any area of my life, especially in the area of my storm? I believe the biggest reason why most people don't want to be corrected or seek out council, and listen to others, is pride. If I had to choose one single thought that hinders people the most in every aspect of their lives, it would be pride, with no exception. Pride says, I don't need any help, I can do this myself, I don't need anyone and I don't need the Bible, I don't need council, don't correct me, cares more about being heard than listening to others, angers easily, impatient, the need to be right, and the list goes on.

Pride also finds ways to justify disobedience to the Lord. I could go on and on with this list, but I think I'll stop here. Why? Because I could write a thousand behaviors here and not one is going to make you change. How do I know this? Because these are the thoughts that have derailed me in my personal, financial, and spiritual life time and time again, and no matter how much I read or saw something on paper, nothing ever seemed to change or get better, until I deliberately made a choice to change my thinking and behavior. You must choose to change then make the proper adjustments that will create that change. The change I'm talking about is spiritual and comes from within, and can only be received through the Holy Spirit - we can't heal ourselves.

"By the power of the Holy Spirit, there must be a change in your thinking and a change in your behavior for a change to take place in your life, PERIOD."

Haughty pride caused Lucifer to fall from heaven before the creation of man. Haughty pride, in its entirety, is summed up in this one sentence: Haughty pride is the wrong attitude of the heart and a haughty spirit, and is the killer of all good things. Romans 12:3 says; "Do not think of yourself more highly than you ought, but rather think of yourself with sober judgment." Arrogant and haughty pride also makes us resistant to being obedient to the Lord. Self-centered pride causes people to think that their happiness, fulfillment, and accomplishments in life come from them, alone. In essence, these types of people have created their own God or have become their own God. Either of these latter options can, and will, have devastating effects on people's lives.

"Haughty pride is a killer of all good things."

Having talked about pride in the negative sense, I believe we must discuss, momentarily, the positive aspect of the word *pride*. For example, I take pride in a job well done, no matter what the task. I don't believe there is anything wrong with getting satisfaction out of our work, loving what we do, and knowing that God blessed us to be as good as we are at whatever it is that we do. Yes, we have had to cultivate our talents, but the Lord created each of us with unique abilities. Without these God-given abilities, we more than likely would not have excelled at whatever it is we do. The Lord gave us these talents; we should make sure to give Him the glory that He deserves, because God doesn't want to share His glory with anyone. It's His and His, alone. There isn't a human on earth who hasn't struggled with pride at some point in life. We are human; and we all mess up from time to time, say things that we wish we hadn't said, and done things that we wish we hadn't done. It's impossible to get it right all the time.

I also don't believe that being saved means we're fixed once and for all and will never say or think a wrong or negative thought again. I do believe, however, that we can learn how to harness these negative thoughts, actions, and emotions, and use them to propel us forward. We need to learn how to deal with the negativity as it comes, but the very first step in overcoming and dealing with any issue with which we are faced is owning up to it and admitting to ourselves that we need help in whatever area we're struggling. Be it fear, pride, trust, jealously, anger, resentment, or un-forgiveness, we all need help when struggling to overcome negative feelings. If we choose to hide our shortcomings and don't admit them, God can't help us with them. Like my good friend, Pastor Jack Valentino, says, you must own it to disown it.

Our short comings and/or sins must be brought into the light of the Lord in order to begin the healing process. We all must be aware of the fact that our pride may get in the way of our taking the first step of admitting our shortcomings. The best way to fight these negative thoughts, actions, and emotions is with the power imbedded in the word of God, the power of the Holy Spirit, and prayer. We must humble ourselves and be so transparent with ourselves and the Lord that we confess everything to Him. God loves us too much to let us stay in the slime pit of pride, and He will take whatever steps necessary to bring this pride to our attention and then pierce our hearts with conviction to get it out.

Final Thoughts

Life comes down to this: Everyone will have trials and tribulations in life. Our ability to overcome these trials and tribulations depends, for the most part, on how we respond to them; and how we respond to them depends, largely, on the degree of our ability to view things from God's perspective. In order to view things from God's perspective, we must have wisdom from Him, and the only way to receive God's wisdom is to study the scriptures, get to know God through them, and ask Him for wisdom each day. Contrary to the popular belief, there is no other way to receive wisdom from the Lord except from the word of God in the Bible and asking Him for it. I highly recommend the book of Proverbs as the best starting place for attaining the wisdom of the Lord. The wisdom of the Lord can unlock the abundant life that we all so desire, if we allow Him to deposit His wisdom in us. We allow Him to impart His wisdom reading and studying His Word and asking Him to bestow it in our lives. No one knows more about us, our circumstances, our lives, and life itself than the one who created life - No one! Once we understand this, why not get plugged into the Almighty God, everlasting Father, and Prince of Peace in Jesus Christ? What are you waiting for? When we live apart from the word of God, we are at odds with Him. When we're at odds with the Lord and want to live life our way, we are, in essence, saying, "BACK OFF GOD; I GOT IT! I KNOW WHAT I'M DOING." Neither, of course, is true.

Chapter Three

The Clock is Ticking

Do you have the time to continue thinking, believing, and living like you always have? You may be saying things are ok and you have no complaints. Please let me say that there's always room for enhancing your life, even for the most content, happy, and successful people. But in order to accomplish this, we're going to have to be very honest with ourselves and begin now. If the Lord chooses to keep us here another day we will be another day older. Every day that goes by, we are also one day closer to death. Sobering thought, isn't it? So why waste precious time spinning our wheels when we don't have to? We must make a decision to change our thinking, thoughts, and overall mindset. When we make the effort to change those things, with the help of the Holy Spirit, in essence, we're changing the direction of our lives; and, typically speaking, we always move toward the direction of our thoughts, especially when we dwell on those thoughts.

The question is, is our desire to stay the same greater than our desire to change? It's important for each of us to ask ourselves the following questions: Why do we keep going back to doing the same things, thinking the same thoughts, and making the same wrong decisions that have brought us nothing but misery, depression, and unhappiness? Why do we continue to participate in the things that always have stolen our love, joy, peace, happiness, and prosperity? Many of us choose to stay in the confines of our comfort zones because doing so allows us to avoid the higher road on which we are called to walk to reach the next plateau that God has for us. Because this higher road calls for a change in our thinking, thoughts, and actions, most people don't want to participate. Every day that we refuse to change for the better, we create a greater distance between ourselves and the purpose God has for us, and we ultimately drive ourselves farther from the truth and from the Lord. I do believe it's God's will for every person to change. God loves us far too much for us to stay the way we are. Change is good; change means growth; and growth is a sign that we're growing closer to God's chosen purpose for our lives. To resist change is to have a prideful attitude, because resisting change says that we are good enough just the way we are. Change will bring us closer to what God wants us to have. The Lord can't give us what he desires for us to have because we're not fit to receive it the way we are. We must change so we can handle God's richest blessings. If we receive it the way we are, we wouldn't know what to do with it. We would mess up the opportunity completely.

"Typically we always move in the direction of our thoughts."

I believe the fundamental reason most people continue to resist change is because, deep within their souls, they're in a crisis of faith and hope. Change requires a leap of faith because change means to leave something familiar then step into the unknown. People who resist change may not believe that changing something will actually change anything. I know, first-hand, that the risk of not changing directions is greater than the risk of changing directions. If you want to change the direction of your life, *YOU must CHANGE the direction of your life*, and only you can make that change. Some people believe they have jumped all the hurdles of life and there are no more hurdles to jump because their lives are not working out the way they would like. In essence, these people are of the opinion that they have done everything possible there is to do. Have you given the reins of your life to the Lord? Do you still have Him in the copilot seat or maybe not in any seat at all? Or are you still trying to live life on your terms, apart from total obedience to the Lord? When our own efforts fail, we adopt a cynical and hopeless attitude that's full of negative thoughts, as well as rebellion. An example of this kind of thinking is found in Isaiah 22:13: "Let us eat and drink…for tomorrow we die." God's chosen people resigned themselves to defeat. In essence, they were saying, "Let's live it up today and do whatever we please, because we're going to die anyway." It's time to rid ourselves of this kind of thinking. It's time to up-root the lack of hope and lack of vision and start believing in a better tomorrow. Let's not lose our purpose for the sake of living for the moment. The Holy Spirit desires to create in us a faith and hope that can ignite His purpose in us, but we must be willing to do our part because He will not do it for us. *Change must be a priority for you.*

"Is God still your co-pilot, and are you still trying to live on your terms?"

Yes, the clock is ticking; and, unfortunately, it's impossible to stop time. The best way to utilize our time is to live by principal instead of preference only, and I say preference only because there is nothing wrong with preference as long as it doesn't separate us from fellowship with the Lord. Most people live by preference instead of principal. We practice what makes us feel good without considering the possible negative effects it could have on us mentally, physically, spiritually, and emotionally. In fact, we are not disciplined or rewarded by what we think is right or wrong, but what the Lord thinks is right or wrong; however, if our thinking is lined up with the Lord through His word, then that's a whole different story. Many times, people will ask a friend's opinion about a certain situation, and if the friend thinks it's ok, or gives the desired answer, then many times that ends the questioning. Many of the people whom we call friends have good intentions. Most of the time, however, these same people are not going to tell us what we need to hear, not because they don't want to tell us, but because they're up to their eyeballs with problems of their own and truly can't see clearly enough through their own mess to help us with ours. The Lord tells us, in Matthew 7:5, "You hypocrite, first take the plank out of your own eye, then you will see clearly to remove the spec from your brothers eye." I'm not going to hit you over the head with this scripture because I think you get it.

"Every day we live, we are one day closer to death."

Why we always try and justify our behavior amazes me. We're frail beings; and we are, for the most part, weak and easy prey, especially when living without the indwelling of the Holy Spirit. We intentionally put ourselves at a distance from Christ when we're disobedient. When standing at a distance from Christ, we are living and walking in darkness. Most people have a tendency to shy away from church and the Lord when they're being disobedient. This is a very shaky way to live because, when our thoughts and behavior are in disagreement with the Lord and His word, it's as if we're going it alone, and as mentioned earlier, it's like we're telling God, "Back off; I got it." Granted, God is always with us and promises to never leave us or forsake us; but, when our thoughts and actions are at odds with the Lord, we're missing God's best for our lives. God will not support our thoughts and behaviors when they are in opposition with His word. The Lord is always there for us, though, and especially when we're ready to be obedient to Him. God will not change His ways to suit anyone. When our thoughts and behaviors are at odds with the Lord, we put Him at a distance. That's not the Lord's choice. Living at a distance from the Lord is no walk in the park, especially for someone who has had a close relationship with Him and then, at some point, got back into the world. There is no substitute for a close relationship with the Lord Jesus Christ, and there is nothing that the world has to offer that can even come close.

There was a time early in my Christian walk when I didn't start and end my day with the Lord. I would go to church on Sunday, and that was the extent of my relationship with God, other than Bible study once a week. During those early years with the Lord, I wasn't walking or thinking like a Christian; and, even later on in my Christian life, I straddled the fence now and then and wasn't where I should have been in relationship with Him. During the first year of my Christian life, it was very difficult to stop thinking the way I was use to thinking. It was also as difficult to stop participating in the things that were of no benefit to me as well. I was living by preference instead of principal. Living by preference, alone, will rob you of all that God has for you and all that He desires to do in and through you. Our true blessings come when we allow God to position us to receive His intended purpose for our lives. God wants to reveal his intended purpose for each of us, but this will never happen if we're always living by preference, apart from the principals of God, and are at odds with Him. In my personal experience, I excluded the Lord from my life when I was living by my personal preference and not considering the Lord in that preference. Whenever I made those kinds of choices, life seemed to be put on hold. The brakes of life would get locked; and, no matter how much I prayed or read my Bible, things would not get better. I was the kid on a merry-go-round, thinking I was going somewhere but not. Why?

Due to my lack of obedience to the Lord, I was out of fellowship with Him. I now believe that my prayers weren't even reaching the ceiling because of my choice to live by preference only. James 4:3 says; "When you ask, you do not receive, because you ask with the wrong motives, that you may spend what you get on your pleasures." My preference was out of line with the word of God; and, I have learned that the times when I have been out of line with the word of God, my motives were out of line with Him as well. When we're out of line with the Lord and His word, we're at odds with God because of our thinking and behavior. This lack of alignment creates static in our communication with Him. The static is caused by sin, and that's the interference that causes us to be insensitive to the Lord's voice, through the Holy Spirit, and also causes our prayers to be hindered as well. Most, if not all of us, know right from wrong; and participating in the wrong thing, especially when we're aware of it, causes us to doubt, have fear, and be uneasy in all we say, do, and think. Also, we become especially uneasy in our relationship with the Lord. The reason we become uneasy is because, deep within our heart of hearts, we know that there is no good thing that can come out of doing a wrong thing. I must admit, off and on for several years, I was living by preference only instead of principal. Living life this way is living for the Lord half-heartedly, at best. Most of us have done this before and can relate to Paul when he says, in Romans 7:15, "I do not understand what I do. For what I want to do I do not do, but what I hate I do". It is so easy for Christians to start thinking and behaving in a way that is unpleasing to the Lord when they don't read and study the word of God. Yes, we all fall short of the glory of God, and we will never be perfect until the Lord takes us home. I must say, though, that reading and studying the word of God on a daily basis is the best thing anyone could possibly do for themselves. The Bible has the most positive, motivational, and life-giving words ever compiled in any book; it's the word of God speaking to us. We must develop the attitude of expectancy from God and not from man; and, in order to do that realistically, we must understand who we are in Him and understand that He wants us to expect from Him. For this to happen, there must be on-going communication, as well as discipline and obedience. God is always willing to speak to us, teach us, guide us, and help us achieve His purpose.

"In order to hear God we must spend time with Him through reading His word and prayer because this is the primary way how God speaks to us"

I believe the biggest reason why the brakes of life lock up on most of us is because there is no communication and/or relationship with the creator of the universe – Father God through Jesus Christ. This is due to having heart trouble; and, of course, I'm not talking about the physical kind but the spiritual kind. The only way to unlock the brakes is to have spiritual heart surgery. I'm not a pastor, psychiatrist, psychologist, or any kind of professional counselor, but what I have learned from my own life experiences is that the condition of one's heart and spirit is the center of most, if not all, issues that prevent us from having peaceful and productive lives and meaningful relationships.

One of the things I've learned is if someone said or did something to hurt you in some way, and you're still hanging on to that thing, it's much worse than your brakes of life being locked up. My friend, you're in prison with shackles on and you're not getting out until you identify the source that triggers your pain and take it to the throne of God through Christ Jesus. Having an unforgiving attitude is one of the most detrimental things that anyone ever could take part in. When you forgive someone for an offense intended toward you, you are, in essence, giving a gift to yourself; because, when you forgive, you free yourself and do no harm to the perpetrator. If, in fact, the accused is guilty of an action against you, the only way that person is going to benefit in any way is to ask for forgiveness from God and show true remorse. If no remorse is shown, there is no true repentance.

I encourage everyone never to hold on to any grievances toward another. God has something special for you and wants to do great things for you and through you, but He will never be able to get it to you or do it through you if you hold on to anger, resentment, and hostility toward another. Many of you reading this book may be thinking to yourself, "I don't feel anger, resentment, or hostility toward anyone." Granted, many people, Christians and non-Christians may not be holding on to any of those feelings, but many people do hold on to such feelings and aren't aware of it. There is such a thing as passive un-forgiveness and passive hostility, and the effects are just as harmful. Sometimes you'll hear people say, "I have forgiven him/her, and I've forgotten all about that incident and don't ever think about it anymore." Then, right after this statement they say – but they need to say they're sorry and apologize. This statement just nullified their forgiveness. Forgiveness has nothing to do with the person who hurt you saying they're sorry. Forgiveness is actually a condition of the heart living out the love that Christ taught, toward the person who hurt you.

Here is a little test to see if there is any un-forgiveness or ill feelings in the form of passive un-forgiveness toward someone. When a certain individual's name comes up in a conversation, how does it make you feel? Do you think about what they did to hurt you? Could you hold an intelligent conversation with that person without having any thoughts of how they have treated you or one of your loved ones? If that person asked you for a favor, and if it was in your power to do it, would you do it peacefully? If, in fact, when you hear the name of that person, does something un-pleasant happen inside you, and are you uncomfortable in the same room with that person? If you can't do some of these things, chances are there's some healing in the form of forgiveness that needs to take place.

Also, for God to get to you what He has for you there must be obedience. God knows about the setbacks and disappointments in your life, and He also knows when you hurt and who hurt you. Here is a very familiar scripture in Romans 12:19 – Do not take revenge, my dear friends, but leave room for God's wrath, for it is written: "it is mine to avenge; I will repay", says the Lord. When we take revenge in the form of un-forgiveness, it leaves no room for the Lord's discipline. If we leave no room for the Lord's discipline because of our un-forgiveness, aren't we, in fact, interfering with something that God Himself may want to do? I believe that is exactly one of the things that the scripture says. Interfering with God's work profits us nothing. There is always a price for participating in the wrong thing, and it doesn't matter what venue it is. Please learn from me. I have participated in enough wrong things in my life to make up for five lifetimes; and, after it was all said and done, I didn't feel any better. I felt worse and was at a greater distance from God and His purpose for my life.

Final Thoughts

Life has its moments of ups, downs, turns, and twists; and, in the process of it all, those ups, downs, turns and twists prevent most of us from living and experiencing an abundant life. Many people, Christians and non-Christians, blame their problems on other people. Then, there are others who blame everything on Satan. Granted, sometimes people and Satan will try to put stumbling blocks in our paths, but we all have the power, via the correct choices and the Holy Spirit, to conquer them and advance to victory. In essence, we are our worst enemies because of our thinking and warped belief system. We must know that there's power in worshiping and praising the Lord Jesus Christ. We must learn that we need to be very honest with ourselves in order for the broken things to be healed in our lives. Time is of the essence, because every day we live brings us one day closer to death. We must be careful how and what we think, because we always move in the direction of our thoughts. God wants us to change because he loves us too much for us to stay the way we are. Change requires a leap of faith. Are you trying to live life on your terms or on God's terms? We are at odds with the Lord when our thoughts and lifestyles are contrary to the word of God. Have you been living by preference only instead of by the principals of God? Have you checked your heart lately – you may need spiritual heart surgery. How is your communication and relationship with the Lord? Have you been spending quality time with the Lord? Are you holding on to any anger, resentment or un-forgiveness? It's impossible for anyone to walk in the will of God while hanging on to anger, resentment, and un-forgiveness.

Chapter Four

The Dark Road: "Satan's Tool Box"

Before I came to know the lord I was on the dark road. I was raised in the Catholic faith and that's all I knew until I came to know Christ as my personal Savior. Please understand, I'm not saying that the Catholic faith is the dark road, I'm simply sharing my background and where some of my spiritual understanding came from. After I came to know the Lord and accepted him as my personal Savior, I attended a Christian Church of the Wesleyan denomination. I thought it was strange that they were not wearing robes as the Catholic priests were. I use to say – they need to wear God's clothes. Yeah right! What are God's clothes? Oh, I now, priestly garments and robes with flowing fabric. That was my perception of what someone in the pulpit should be wearing. That's the way I was raised. I never really knew about being obedient to Christ, reading the Bible, and praise and worship in the sense I know it now. I viewed God like my parents viewed God – that's a scary thought when I think about it. Why? Because there was no talk about the need to praise and worship the Lord, reading, studying, and memorizing the Bible, being diligent in sacrificial giving, honoring God with tithes and offerings, attending

Church services regularly, and having that one on one personal relationship with the only true God in the universe – Jesus Christ.

Have you ever thought about why you believe, think, and behave the way you do?

Many people pursue a god that fits into their lifestyle, instead of the true God of the Bible. They think, "This is the way I see God, so this is the way He must be." They try to interweave secular views with some twisted views of their own and think, "This must be from God, so this is the way God must be." Most people want God to agree with them and fit in with what they think is right and true, instead of believing in what the Lord knows and has determined what is right and true. This is one of the main reasons why our country is in a moral sewer - the Dark Road. There are some who have also created their own belief system. I once ran across an article in which a woman was suggesting that her husband write a book on how to create your own belief system. What a scary thought!

I believe the biggest reason why people create their own belief system, rather than believe in the Bible, is because the Bible does not fit in with their lifestyle. Most people choose how they want to live, and then build a belief-system around that; this is truly the dark road. There also are those who say that they're spiritual but not religious. Typically what they mean when they say they're not religious is, "I don't go to church; I don't go along with organized religion; I don't believe that God wrote the Bible - men wrote it and put their own twist on it; it's not necessary to attend church; and so on. Here's one I get a kick out of: I heard one of the daytime talk show hosts say that God doesn't judge, people do. Yes, people do judge and I agree that that's wrong. The Bible says that all judgment has been given to the Son; so, you better believe that God judges, and He will be the final judge and jury one day. The people who believe that God doesn't judge have never been saved by the grace of God; they never have accepted His one and only son, who died on the cross as a symbol of his love and as repayment for their sins. These are the people who rarely, if ever, open the Bible and study the word of God. These are the same people who say that there is no such thing as Satan or sin, and there is no such place as Hell. In short, these people are saying that the Bible is a fake and Christ is too. These types of thoughts truly lead down a dark road.

"People who don't believe in the Bible don't believe in it because it doesn't fit in with their lifestyle."

These are the same people who believe that everyone is going to go to heaven and live with the Lord for all eternity. Yes, these are the people who say, "I'm spiritual but not religious." Granted, being religious like the Pharisees of the Bible is not a good thing. But the point I want to make here is that people who claim to be spiritual but not religious don't understand that it's impossible to be spiritual without the indwelling of the Holy Spirit. Here, again, they believe that everyone has the Holy Spirit in them. This is so untrue! It's ridiculous even to think such a thing. If a person does not believe that Christ was born of the Virgin Mary, died on the cross for the final sacrifice of sin for all who believe in Him, and if he or she does not believe that Christ rose from the dead on the third day and is now seated at the right hand of the Father, this person is not indwelt with the Holy Spirit. There is no chance for that person to be with the living God when he or she makes the final departure from this earth - period. Allah, Muhammad, and Buddha did not die for anyone and are just mere humans and are still dead. The Lord says in Jn.16:7, Nevertheless I tell you the truth; It is expedient for you that I go away: for if I do not go away, the Comforter will not come unto you; but if I depart, I will send him unto you. There you have it - Jesus is the one who sends the Holy Spirit to dwell in you. Why in the world would Jesus send His Holy Spirit to dwell inside a person if that person doesn't believe in him? And what I mean by believing in him is this - that, Jesus is the only way possible to get to heaven when we leave this earth, and that we must be born again believers to get there – PERIOD! If the Holy Spirit truly has residence in someone, they would be convicted of so many things that they now perceive as being ok, especially that he "Jesus" is the only way and there is no other. These people just don't understand the Holiness of the Lord, and how He doesn't like to look upon sin, but then here we go again - they don't think there is such a thing as sin. This is truly the dark road. The farther we drift from God and the word of God, the more confused "dark" our thinking becomes. When we fail to learn from our past failures, future failure is inevitable. When we intentionally forget a lesson learned, we risk repeating the same mistake over and over again. Your past is your school of experience. If your past is not pointing you to the Lord and His word - your thinking is out of line with the Lord's thinking.

The only way to truly change the direction of your life is to change the road you're on. People who are not indwelt with the Holy Spirit cannot understand scripture; it is nonsense to them. 1 Corinthians 2:14 says, "The man without the Spirit does not accept the things that come from the Spirit of God, for they are foolishness to him, and he cannot understand them, because they are spiritually discerned". There are two types of people. People who are born-again believers - who are indwelt with the Holy Spirit, and people who are not born-again believers - who are not indwelt with the Holy Spirit. People who are indwelt with the Holy Spirit have the ability, and can discern the spiritual things of the Bible because they are born of the Spirit and are spiritually discerning. It's the Holy Spirit that enables us to understand, draw close to, and love the scriptures. The natural man who is not a born-again believer cannot understand the spiritual things of the Bible because he is not indwelt with the Holy Spirit. That's why people who are not indwelt with the Holy Spirit think the word of God is not from God - they are not spiritually discerning. It's impossible for them to operate out of the Spirit because they don't possess the Holy Spirit.

"Change your thinking, change your vocabulary, and change your habits. Get in line with the word of God, and your life will be changed forever."

This concept sounds like a lot, doesn't it? It is if we try to change and re-direct our lives on our own, within our own perceived power. Achieving this type of change is truly impossible without the power of the Holy Spirit, and that's why most people haven't made any significant and positive changes in their lives. Most people still use the same vocabulary they used when they were teenagers. They act the same way, believe the same way, think the same thoughts, and still are in the same habits, as well. Why is this so? The answer is simple: If people don't have the power of the Holy Spirit living in them, it's impossible for them to hear the true voice of the living God in Christ Jesus. If the Holy Spirit was truly living in them, they would be convicted of their sin because that's how the Lord works his cleansing and healing. He convicts us in our spirits to let us know that we are on the wrong path of life. There must be a conviction that something is wrong before any change can take place. The first step in working toward this change is that you must be born-again in the sense that you ask Christ to forgive you for your sins and ask Him into your heart, and accept Him as your personal Savior; then and only then, does the Holy Spirit take up residence inside of you. As you read and study the Bible, the Lord will reveal himself to you in ways you never imagined. It's so vital to get spiritually right with the Lord. If we're not spiritually right with God, we're viewing him and the world through spiritually sick eyes and interpreting life with a spiritually sick mind, therefore making it literally impossible to see God as he truly is. Instead, we see him in a way that fits in with the lifestyle that we have chosen to live. I must point out that our spiritually sick eyes come from our spiritually sick heart. When our heart is not right with the Lord, it affects every area of our lives, especially when it comes to falling for the lies of Satan. The Bible says that Satan came to kill, steal, and destroy, and he will do just that if we allow him. He also will try to keep us linked up to the things that are holding us back. When we look at God with spiritually sick eyes, we see Him as a higher power which we all have heard some talk about - or "the man upstairs." I've even seen articles with God spelled like this – g-d. People who use these kinds of spellings for God and shun him by calling him the man upstairs or a higher power, are not connected and in a relationship with the true living God in Christ Jesus. He's the Christ, the Savior, the everlasting Father, the prince of peace, and He becomes very personal to you. Christ was fully man and is fully God. Father God put himself as a seed in the womb of the Virgin Mary; and, before Jesus was born (Luke 1:31) Father God named him Jesus. Jesus was God in human flesh. Isaiah 9:6 says it this way - "For to us a child is born, to us a son is given, and the government will be on his shoulders. And he will be called Wonderful Counselor, Mighty God, Everlasting Father, Prince of

Peace". God came to us in human form so we could have a way to have a personal relationship with him. We need to acknowledge the God who dwells in Christ Jesus and who wants a walking, talking, praising, and worshiping relationship with us. Without that kind of relationship with Christ, we can never really please God and get to know him personally, and that's just what the Lord wants: to have a personal relationship with us. Most people who don't like to attend church, read their Bibles, pray, and have a walking, talking, relationship with God perceive Christ as someone who will interfere with their lives, instead of pointing them in a direction that is best for them. They see God and the church as a hindrance instead of a way to better their lives. This is truly the dark road. They don't see Jesus as the person who was fully man and fully God. They don't see Jesus as the Lord of their lives. When Jesus is truly the Lord of people's lives, they will want to spend quality time with Him and learn as much about Him as they possibly can.

"We will never see God the way he intended us to see Him as long as we're looking at him with spiritually sick eyes and a spiritually sick heart."

These people don't perceive there is sin in their lives, because they don't believe in sin. They think all is well with God. They say, "God is not going to hurt me because He's a God of love, and he loves me." Yes, the Lord is a God of love; and he does love all, but what people are missing when they only see the loving side of God is that the Lord hates sin and will not tolerate sin and especially His children living in sin. The Bible says that God is slow to anger, which means that He is amazingly patient with us, but then there comes a time when the Lord says, "Enough is enough," and then the hammer comes down. The Lord always chooses the discipline that fits the sin.

Guess what, though: We can prevent the hammer by choosing obedience. It's impossible for us to function the way God intended when we're in opposition to the laws He set in place. We all try to hide our sin; and yes, I'm talking about Christians as well, and especially Christians because we're supposed to know better. There are many who live under the guise of the word Christian. As a close friend of mine puts it, they talk "Christianeez;" but, in reality, they live rotten to the core when no one is watching. Most of us, at some point in our lives, have had secret, un-confessed sin in our lives. I have strolled into places that I should never have strolled into and never have shared that with anyone until I confessed it to my then wife when we were in marriage counseling and going through a divorce. As I'm writing this book, the Lord just impressed upon my heart that this secret behavior caused me to be blind as to what was going on in my wife's social life and at work, and that's all I'm going to say about that. That's a whole other book, and yes I will be writing that very soon. Yes she was up to no good, but so was I. Her sin was no worse than mine. In any case, secret sins will cause a person to be blinded to the Lord's truths in more ways than you could ever imagine. These secret things that we keep to ourselves can never be removed if we keep thinking thoughts like, "it's ok to do them," "God doesn't care," "I'm not hurting anyone," and so on. Our ability, apart from Christ, to be delivered from any hindrance is impossible. It may appear that such secrets and the hindrances they cause are gone, and they may be gone for a while, but it won't be long before they return, stronger and more unbearable than before. Don't be fooled and taken in by many of the new age books out there that talk about the universe, the ego, and a higher power. They have a bunch of sayings that make zero sense and never give the glory to the Lord Jesus Christ for the healing. All healing comes through the sacrificial blood of the Lord Jesus, and we owe it to the Lord to verbally give him all the glory, honor, and praise, for all the healing in our lives. I don't recommend that you spend your hard-earned money on new age books. If these books don't mention the cross, the broken body and the blood of our Lord Jesus Christ, then don't waste your hard earned money or time reading them. I have browsed through several of these new age books and found that they take a majority of their content from the Bible and twist it to make it sound like their own; that's plagiarism at its best. Yes, I have taken the liberty to investigate many of the new age books out there. I won't name them here, but many of the authors of these books don't believe there are things such as sin, Satan, and hell. God said in John 3:16: "for God so loved the world that he gave his only begotten son, that whosoever believes in him shall not parish but have everlasting life. Is Jesus a lunatic and a liar, or is he telling the truth? I say he's telling the truth. Those people who have been writing that there's no such thing as sin, Satan, and hell are actually calling God a liar because God says that there are such things as sin, Satan, and hell. The spirit of anti-Christ cannot tolerate the company of the Spirit of Christ, and this is why Satan uses the New Age movement - to separate people from Christ, his blood, the cross, and the living Word of God in the Bible. This is truly the dark road.

Any person, and all other religions who say, we don't believe that Christ is the only way to get to heaven, we have our own belief and our own way to get to heaven – they are actually telling the Heavenly Father who sent His son to die for all humanity that, He messed up. They are saying to God that He made a mistake – you didn't need to send Jesus to die on the cross – "LOOK" we have found a way to get to where you are without Jesus. Do you see how silly this is? This is blasphemy at best. Just writing this statement, and then reading it afterwards – gives me the creeps.

"We must believe that Christ is who he says he is."

Many of the people who have been elected to public office have been doing a good job at taking God out of our country, our schools, our work places, and out of most public buildings, as well. When disaster comes, however, who's the first name they call on? You got that right - God! The Lord is pretty close to being completely out of America because, in a nation obsessed with political correctness, it's politically correct to say, "We don't want to hurt anyone's feelings, and we don't want to offend anyone." Why is it that they don't care about hurting the Lord God? Yes, it's always nice to please people if we can, but surely not at the expense of displeasing the Lord. Government dictates that we can't talk about the Lord in our schools any more, but it's ok to talk about evolution. This is truly the dark road. Don't fall for this trash, because this is garbage at its best. As real men and women, we, need to step up to the plate, confront these false teachings, stop worrying about offending someone, and start pleasing the Lord. As mentioned earlier, our country is in a moral sewer, and the leaders of our country have not helped matters much. Of course, we are all accountable for the moral decisions that we make; however, when we have a government that agrees to put into law the things that are contrary to the word of God, this surely works against all believers, and our country as a whole. Our so-called system is so messed up from the law makers, we don't really have a system any more, at least not the one on which our country was founded and based on. At the time of this writing some are saying that we are not just a Christian nation any more, but are a Christian, Muslim, and every-other-religion-under-the-sun nation. That's messed up and is truly the dark road. We are a Christian nation and nothing else.

We need to be God pleasers, as opposed to people pleasers.

Just because we as a nation have allowed others to come and worship as they please, does not change the fact that our country was built upon the typical Christian values, and does not change the fact that we are a Christian nation. Please don't take offense to my statement, and I mean no harm to other religions as well. I'm ok with others worshiping as they please, but we who are of the Christian faith and/or are, indeed, true Americans need to take a stand because our politicians have been making it better and easier for the other religions of the world to worship how they choose, and making it harder for us of the Christian faith to worship how we choose; this is my main concern, here. We should not have to change the way things have been since the founding of our nation just because people of other faiths decide to live in our country. If we, as Christians, decided to live in the countries that are not of the Christian faith, and start to complain about how they worshipped and started to protest saying you shouldn't do this or that, how far do you think we would get?

The Spirit of anti-Christ cannot tolerate the company of the Spirit of Christ.

God is the same today as he was five thousand years ago, and the problems that he had with the people back then, are still very present today. What's that, you ask? Well, I won't go into detail, here, because that would be a complete book in and of itself, but please read some books of the Old Testament, like Leviticus, Numbers, Deuteronomy, Judges, 1st and 2nd Samuel, and Jeremiah, and you will see how the people and their leaders took God out of their lives and out of the country, and you will see how God dealt with them because of it. We always blame everything on the economy and many other things; but if you really study the scriptures, you'll see that it was the Lord who pulled the carpet out from under our country's feet because of their false idol worship and the way they were living. We are actually doing very similar things today in our country, through the leaders who are taking the true and only living God out of everything. The moral principles of our country are gone.

Yes, the Lord is letting our country worsen because of the way our leaders have taken him out of everything just so they can be politically correct and not offend anyone. This is biblical – read the Bible. We are reaping exactly what we have sown. I believe this with all my heart: All of the people who are in charge of making decisions and policy changes in our country and are living contrary to the word of God will be fully accountable to God when they face him on that final day. I believe that this is the main reason why our country is in a moral and financial sewer, and this is truly the dark road. Most people say, "I can do as I please." Here's what they think in a nut shell: "You go to church, and I don't. You are always reading your Bible and I don't even own one. You praise and worship the Lord and I don't. You're doing all of these things and yet my life is just as fruitful or more so than yours is." They also may be thinking, "I make more money than you, I have a bigger house than you do, and I drive nicer cars and take better vacations than you do, and yet I don't read the Bible or go to Church." So they think, "I must be ok with God, and he must approve of my lifestyle and belief system." There are multi–millionaires and billionaires who are confessed atheists; so this blows that theory. This is worth repeating: God is slow to anger. He's patiently waiting for all to turn from their distasteful and sinful ways and fully repent and turn to Him. So what is repentance? Repentance means two very important things. It not only means changing your ways, but changing your mind as well. Romans 12:1-2 says, "Therefore, I urge you, dear brothers and sisters, in view of God's mercy, to offer your bodies as living sacrifices, holy and acceptable to God; this is your spiritual act of worship. Do not conform any longer to the pattern of this world, but be transformed by the renewing of your mind. Then you will be able to approve what God's will is – his good, pleasing, and perfect will." This is not something you try, but it's a way of life. We must purposefully change our minds in order to change our ways. Why is it so hard for us as believers to stop doing the things that separate us from the Fellowship of the Lord? I believe it's because we haven't really tapped into the power of the resurrection of Christ. But we can't tap into that power while living in habitual and willful sin and thinking that it's ok with God. For many of us, because of the way we live, it appears as if we really don't believe that the Lord is alive and well and that he's aware of all that we do. We live as if God doesn't know our lifestyle, our way of thinking, and our daily thoughts. How dumb is that!

"Most people say, 'I can do as I please' and believe there are no consequences for their actions. THIS IS TRULY THE DARK ROAD."

There's a big difference between someone doing things that the Lord doesn't approve of while thinking that it's ok with him and having no remorse, while someone else is doing the same things that the Lord doesn't approve of but, this person believes that it's wrong and is continually asking God for help and is wanting to change their behavior and thinking. I'm not saying that it's less wrong and surely not saying that it's a license to sin, but what I am saying is - the person who agrees with the Lord that the lifestyle they're living is sin and truly has remorse and is wanting to change is already on their way to a changed behavior because their thinking has been changed through the conviction of the Holy Spirit. In retrospect, the other person doesn't even want to change because they don't perceive that their lifestyle and behavior is sin. They think everything is ok with their lifestyle. There's a huge difference here and believe me, the Lord does know the difference between the two different hearts and minds - He can't be fooled. The Lord knows when people have true remorse and are truly sorry for their sins, but that's only the beginning. The Lord wants us to come full-circle with our disobedience to Him and repent. When we're separated from the fellowship of the Lord, it's like being locked in a soundproof booth and trying to have a conversation with someone outside that booth. That's not possible now, is it? This is why it's of the utmost importance to repent from sin and abstain from all intentional sin. I know there are times when things may seem impossible; but, many times, God will ask us to do something so hard that we may perceive it as impossible. God works this way because when we conquer the seemingly impossible, He wants us to know that it was definitely a miracle from Him, and not because of our own capability, efforts, or smarts; rather, our success comes from Him and because of Him. God receives all the glory. I made a statement earlier that God is not real to some people. Here's a question to ponder: Remember the last time you did something that made the Lord unhappy? Remember when you said a horrible thing about another person? Whatever the case may be, if it was something you said or did, it doesn't matter; but my question is, if the Lord was physically present just before you said or did that certain thing, would you have said or done it? I believe everyone would say, "Of course not." If Christ was a physical guest in your home, would you still act, talk, and behave the way you typically do? The truth is, Christ is in your house, and he's aware of everything that you say, do, and think. Please know that I'm talking about myself, as well. I must admit that I have lived as if my sin was hidden from the Lord. How dumb is that? Just as Christ says you will know a tree by its fruit, you can also tell what's inside people's hearts by what comes out of their mouths and the way they live and act; that's the fruit. Christ is alive and well, and He is always present via the Holy Spirit. Christ is always with the born-again Christian through the Holy Spirit; and yes, when any child of God sins, we take the Lord right through the mess with us, and He sees and hears everything, as if he is physically present. Yes, He is that real and that present!

Final Thoughts

It's of the utmost importance to know not only the reason but also the basis behind your beliefs. What is the basis of your beliefs? Who do you say Jesus is? Is Jesus a liar or a lunatic, or is he telling the truth when he says no one can come unto the Father except by him? I say he's telling the truth, and he is who he says he is. If you're one who believes that the Holy Spirit lives in all people, even if they haven't accepted Christ as their savior, what's your basis for that belief? Do you have anything concrete to base that on, or does this belief just fit your lifestyle? Do you actually have a walking, talking, obedient lifestyle with the creator of the universe; and, if you think so, how are you achieving it? How have you been praising and worshiping the Lord? Do you ever think about why your vocabulary and thinking hasn't changed over the years? That might be something to look into. Secret sins...do you have any? Is Christ real to you? What would you do and how would you act if Christ was physically present with you all the time? Have you ever thought about the real reasons why our country is in a moral and financial sewer? Have you ever studied the Old Testament to see how the Lord dealt with the leaders and the countries themselves when they took the true God out of everything? Have you considered that you possibly could have brought some, if not most, of your problems upon yourself because of your belief system and behavior? Have you ever wanted to do something that you didn't think you could ever accomplish? With God, all things are possible. Sometimes the Lord will ask you to do the impossible just so you can know that it was all because of Him that you succeeded; not because of you alone. We must know that there is power in praising and worshiping the Lord Jesus Christ.

Chapter Five

Get Bitter or Better - The Choice is Yours

For most of us, it's easy to have a good attitude if no one else is in the room. I say *most of us* because there are those who, even when they're alone, they have a bad attitude. I've met a few of those kinds of people, haven't you? If we would take the time to look at the God-given abilities and blessings we already have and be thankful for them, there's every possibility that our grumbling would come to a halt. I sat down one night and wrote down the things for which I'm grateful. My blessings became very apparent to me. If you woke up this morning, you're blessed. If you're breathing, you're blessed. If you can see, hear, and speak, you're blessed. If you can do any one of those things, you're blessed. Now, this is not to say that many of the wonderful people who aren't able to do some of those things are not blessed. They are truly blessed as well. I'm just using the things mentioned above as examples.

There are so many things in life that we use, and many things that we do on a daily basis that we don't even think about because we take them for granted. Have you ever stopped to think about all the people who are not able to do some of those things - the things that we take for granted? I believe one of the reasons why we don't think about these everyday blessings of ours is because most of what we do in our everyday lives is routine, and we go about our daily activities without giving it any thought. Another reason we may not be as thankful as we should is because many of us are so bogged down with our past hurts, suppressed anger, resentment, and un-forgiveness from those hurts, that it leaves little room for anything else. When we have our hearts filled with these kinds of things, there is no room for gratitude, thankfulness, and the true love for others and of life that the Lord wants us to have.

My father was in the hospital several years ago for heart surgery, and he lost circulation in one leg, which led to an amputation. Throughout the whole experience, I never heard him complain or get upset about it. From the day he found out he had to have surgery, until the day of his death, my dad's attitude and disposition remained positive; it never wavered. What a testimony! My father was saved late in his life and never really had an opportunity to learn Christian principals properly and experience abundant life in Christ. That being said, my dad was not aware of how a Christian should love, accept, and forgive; he just did it because that's just the way he was. Love, acceptance, and forgiveness have always come easy for my dad. He truly was the best man I have ever known. Several years ago, I saw an interview with Ray Charles on *60 minutes*. Some of you may have seen it. Leslie Stahl asked Mr. Charles, "Do you ever get mad because of your blindness?" Rays response was, "What is there to be mad about?" He said seeing is about 1/99th of what life is all about. It's possible he had moments of distress about having no sight; that, I don't know. If he did, that's just what they were: moments. He made a choice not to not have a victim's mentality. Quincy Jones said that Ray Charles knew how to convert his pain to joy and his darkness to light. That reminds me of a certain scripture that talks about an upright person who walks with God, and it goes like this: "Even in darkness light dawns for the upright, for the gracious and compassionate and righteous man" (Psalm 112:4). If you were in a situation where darkness was about to overtake you, and then all of a sudden, light came bursting in to save you, wouldn't that be awesome?

That's just the kind of God that we have in Christ Jesus. We must realize that the past is the past, and we can't undo the unfortunate things that came our way. Instead, we must realize that we can do something about our today and our tomorrow, because the decisions we make today will shape our tomorrow; but remember: we are not guaranteed a tomorrow, so, let's live everyday like it's our last. Only you can make a decision to remove the shackles and not be a prisoner of your past or the misfortunes that life has brought you. We don't have to be imprisoned by bitterness, anger, or an unforgiving attitude. The best way to live in a state of thankfulness, as well as releasing the shackles of anger, resentment, and un-forgiveness, is to praise and worship the Lord. When we praise God, this is not only an expression of our reverence and worship to Him, but also a way of expressing our faith and trust in Him. God responds to praise and worship and actually releases the power of the Holy Spirit to work in our circumstances when we praise and worship Him. The power of the Holy Spirit is the only way to receive healing from our past hurts, as well as bitterness, anger, and un-forgiveness.

"Praising the Lord should be a way of life because he deserves it and there's power in praise."

One of the things that praise does is, it lets God know that we trust him with everything that goes on in our lives, no matter the situation. If we only praise the lord when things are good and going our way, we're not showing any kind of faith or trust. Church and/or corporate praise and worship are a very small, but integral, part of the Christian relationship with the Lord. Some people may not have a church where they can praise and worship the Lord each week; and if that's the case, I think you really need to look into exactly why you feel the way you do about church. I'm not in favor of neglecting church, and I must say that people are not Christians because they go to church; rather, they go to church because they're Christians. Fish love to swim, birds love to fly, and Christians go to church because it's one of the things that we love to do, and the Holy Spirit draws us there because that's where He wants us to be. As mentioned, corporate worship is a small but integral part of worship. I say small because people go to church just one or two days a week, as compared to seven days a week. Praise and worship can be a state of mind and heart, throughout the day, seven days a week. One of the things I've heard people say about not wanting to go to church is there's way too many hypocrites in there. My thought is, "Well, you'll be in good company. Just walk on in, one more won't hurt." There may be some hypocrites in church today; and to be very honest, I think we all have been hypocritical at some point in our Christian walk.

I have a relationship with Christ not because I'm good, but because I am *not* good and have fallen short of the glory of God. He rescued me from myself and the ruin I was causing. But He's changing me. I'm still a mess, but I'm God's mess. If, in fact, you do attend church on a regular basis, I'm hoping that you're not waiting until Sunday to praise and worship the Lord. Corporate praise and worship are great things, but that's not your personal one-on-one relationship with the Lord and should not be a replacement for, but an addition to, what you're already doing throughout the week; it's all about how you are with Him Monday through Saturday, as well. You can worship at home every morning when you get up, and just before you go to bed, or while driving in your car, and throughout the day. You get the idea? It's not where and how you praise and worship the Lord that's important, but it is important that you *do* praise and worship Him. With that being said, I firmly believe that praising, worshiping, and talking to the Lord on-the fly should not be our only time of doing so. In other words, sometimes we can get in such a hurry that we say to ourselves, "I can pray while driving to work." That's good; and please continue to do so; but let's not let that be the only time that we do pray and have fellowship with the Lord outside of church. In my humble opinion, the best of all scenarios is to set some time aside, go to a place where there's no distraction, and hunker down with the Lord. Praising and worshiping the Lord should be a way of life because of who He is. He is surely worthy of it, and there's healing power attached to praise and worship.

"We must re-condition our minds
by renewing our minds."

I'm not a body builder, but I have been weight training most of my adult life; and I would like to use this experience as an analogy, if I may, please. We all know or have heard at some time or another about the effects that weight training and cardio exercise have on our health. It strengthens our heart, lungs, muscles, and overall skeletal system, and it keeps us in a better state of well-being. We can condition our minds and train our thinking in the same manner. During my training, I have experienced significant gains, as well as setbacks. Gains come from exercising on a consistent basis throughout the week and maintaining a diet of proteins, carbohydrates, and fats. Many times, setbacks come when training, and diet takes a back seat to the other things a person needs to do in life. It's all about setting priorities and balancing both. So, what does all this stuff about exercising have to do with mind conditioning, you ask? Conditioning our minds works in a similar fashion as exercising our muscles and putting good nutrition in our bodies; however, instead of lifting weights and eating right, we are exercising our minds with good, wholesome thoughts and, most of all, feeding our minds with the word of God. We must take a proactive role and choose to start thinking differently. When we keep feeding our minds with only sinful and negative thoughts, only sinful and negative experiences will come into our lives. Remember the old saying, "Garbage in, garbage out?" This saying is still so true. The Lord says, in Galatians 6:7-8, "Be not deceived; God cannot be mocked. A man reaps what he sows. The one who sows to please his sinful nature, from that nature will reap destruction; the one who sows to please the Spirit, from the Spirit will reap eternal life."

So, now that we know that our minds can be trained in a similar fashion to our muscles, just how do we do that? I believe the first step is to memorize and begin applying Romans 12:2, which says, "Do not conform any longer to the pattern of this world, but be transformed by the renewing of your mind." Then, you will be able to test and approve what God's will is – his good, pleasing and perfect will. So, how do we renew that mind of ours? Practice, practice, practice! Will we get it right the first time?

More than likely, not, but don't stop there. When you fall, just get back up, dust yourself off, and begin again. Just be persistent in making the needed changes. First and foremost, it's impossible to accomplish this task without the power of the Holy Spirit – PERIOD! You must stay connected to the Lord through prayer and worship, along with reading, memorizing and meditating on the word of God. In my personal experience, I have found that the only way I can stay truly connected to God is making two important decisions. The first of the two decisions is, making a change in my thinking; this had to be my first priority, because the second decision will never happen if change is not a priority. The second decision is to practice, consistently, at making the change. This decision calls for active participation. The practice I'm talking about is very similar to learning how to play an instrument or learning a new job skill; either requires repetition of that particular behavior, action, or attitude.

In my late teens and early twenties, I was a drummer in a Rock-N-Roll Band; and I had to practice, even when I didn't feel like it. I recall pounding on my mother's pots and pans with spoons when I was five or six years old. Did it help? You bet it did. I got the idea from my dad. He used to play the spoons, and he played them very well. I first learned how to keep rhythm by beating on mom's pots and pans. I drove my mom bananas, and my parents bought me my first drum set when I was about seven years old. It was a kid set, of course, but a drum set, nevertheless. I remember my cousin Mitch sketching the name "RJ and the GTO's" on the front of the bass drum head. I thought that was the coolest thing - I'll never forget it. We had vinyl records back then, and my sisters had stacks of them. I use to play my drums while listening to their music; and, before long, I learned many of the songs. Later, when I was seventeen years old, I formed my first real band. This was a real wake-up call for me, in terms of playing with consistency and stamina, as well as learning somewhere around sixty songs. I recall rehearsing certain songs for hours and hours with the band, then rehearsing for many more hours in my own time. I would then continue to replay those songs in my head, while working and doing almost every activity as well. I share this with you because the same tenacity and practice that it takes to become a good musician, get in great shape, or learn a new job skill; will train your thinking as well. You must actively take a roll in your decision-making and conclude that your thinking hasn't done the job thus so far; then, choose to make change a priority, and discipline yourself to do the necessary work to make the change. We must choose to actively participate for any change to take place. Is this an easy thing to do? Definitely not, and that's why most of us haven't accomplished it yet. If you're of the opinion that your thinking doesn't need adjusting at times, you just may have discovered one of your biggest obstacles. You may have to re-think this issue, bring it to the Lord in prayer, and ask Him to reveal the things in your thinking that may be obstacles standing in the way of your progress in all endeavors of life.

We must bathe ourselves in prayer and the word of God, and I'm talking about saturating our minds with scripture, prayer, praise, and worship. Please pardon me, because what I'm about to say may not feel good to you, but it is another area that needs some attention from all of us. Most of us think that we have it all together and are on the right track; but, in reality, we are really messed up. I've been there, done that, and you're no different than I and most people. If you haven't done any kind of work to get through your issues and get to the root of them, then, more than likely, you are still hanging on to some anger, resentment, and un-forgiveness, as well as other things that only a true professional can identify. I want to clarify, that when I say the word work, I'm not saying we are healed or fixed in any way because of what we do. The word work in this sense is actively taking a proactive role in making the decision to get some help. Yes this does take some work on our part because it's not always easy admitting our issues and becoming transparent for someone to see.

Our healing comes from the Lord – not from anything that we do.

Here's another area of our thinking that needs attention. We are always trying to analyze what's going on in our friends' lives; and, boy, do we have all the answers. We offer our advice as quick as lightning, even if our friends don't want to hear what we have to say; and yes, I have been guilty of this as well, and am learning to hold my tongue instead of being Mr. Counselor. But I will always point someone in the direction of the Lord, first; and, if the Lord prompts me, I will recommend some sort of counseling. It's very easy to recognize when someone has anger, resentment, and un-forgiveness issues; and, as the Lord leads, I may point that out to someone, if I have a close relationship with him or her. A scripture comes to mind from the seventh chapter of Matthew, verses 3 through 5, with which you may be familiar, and it's worth repeating here: "Why do you look at the speck in your brother's eye, but do not notice the log that is in your own eye?

Or how can you say to your brother, let me take the speck out of your eye, and behold, the log is in your own eye? You hypocrite, first take the log out of your own eye, and then you will see clearly to take the speck out of your brothers eye" We're always so quick to tell others about the right and wrong way to do things, the right and wrong way to believe, and the list goes on. If you've done a lousy job with your own affairs, how in the world can you council somebody else? The Lord says you can't get your own life straightened out, so stop trying to counsel others and take care of your own junk. This is one of the critical areas where we need to re-train our thinking. I understand; you've read a book or two and have taken a class or two; now, you're a counselor, right? Not so! Over the past thirty years, I've taken many Prayer Deliverance classes and read approximately one hundred motivational and self-help books along with the greatest book ever published: the Holy Bible. This surely doesn't qualify me as a counselor and surely doesn't qualify me to give any advice whatsoever. I must say, again, that I don't like giving advice; but I also don't have a problem directing someone toward the Lord and some good counseling, as the Lord directs. So, I believe the best of all scenarios is to stop being a counselor to your friends, and just listen to them and pray for them.

Going back to what we were talking about earlier, we must train our minds to refrain from moaning and groaning, singing the somebody-done-me-wrong song, and trying to counsel our friends, because, actually, by doing so, we become somewhat of a thorn in their side, as well as possibly interfering with what the Lord wants to do in their lives. I have learned the best thing to do when it comes to friends is to point them in the right direction, and anything beyond that is a waste of your time and theirs. If they receive your direction, great; if not, don't worry about it, but keep them in prayer and move on. Always be there for them and be a good listener and friend. I know: It's hard to hold our tongues at times, and I'm getting much better at it myself. Just think, "They got themselves in their own mess, just as most of us have, and in no way are we going to get them out of it. Remember, they're not your children, so stop talking to them as if they were. I shared this issue about the counseling of our friends because more than likely you may be making your friend grumble and complain about you when he leaves your presence, or after you got off the phone – and you wouldn't want that.

We haven't a clue what others may be going through.

On to another sticky area where most of us have problems: Somewhere down the road, at some point in time, everyone runs into an angry, bitter, or hostile individual; it's just a fact of life. When this happens, how are we supposed to act? First of all, we must realize that we have no idea what is going on in this person's life and what it's like to walk in their shoes. Secondly, don't strike back with bitterness, because you'll just be pouring gas on an already huge fire, which will turn into an inferno. How do I know? I know this because I have been guilty of striking back myself, and I know, first-hand, that it never accomplishes anything. You may have come into contact with someone who just has experienced something tragic in his life or has had an on-going, difficult situation with which he's been dealing with.

More than likely, this person is seeking love and acceptance, as well as someone to just listen. If you strike back, you will be aiding him in going somewhat deeper into what he already is experiencing. So, just handle the situation with love; you will be glad you did, and so will he. Also more than likely, somewhere in your past you have been that hostile person who someone met – whether face-to-face or in your car, right? We all have the power to choose to respond to everyone in a kind way; and if, for some reason, we can't do this, then it's possible that there are some issues in our own lives that need some attention. Now, I understand that there may be some situations where we need to defend ourselves and our loved ones; that's a given. If someone tries to lay his hands on you or me in a hostile fashion, that's a different situation. It's natural to defend ourselves; and, if we are able to walk away without fighting, that's the best defense of all. Then there's another scenario: If anyone tried to hurt my daughters, grandchildren, or any of my loved ones, physically, in my presence, I definitely would stand up to whomever and protect my family. That's an entirely different set of circumstances than the topic of this chapter, but it's worth sharing because everyone who's able to protect himself and his loved ones would do exactly that: protect them.

Okay, now that we have that settled, let's briefly talk about how to handle confrontation. First of all, let's not go on the defense. Unless you're being physically attacked, then of course you should defend yourself the best way you know how - that is, if you're physically able to. I never would suggest that someone sit there and take a beating from anyone. Secondly, even if we don't know the first thing about the other party, we do know how to press his or her buttons, don't we? It comes naturally for most of us to say the wrong thing at the wrong time, and that's the flesh working at its best. For example, let's not be sarcastic and try to demean another's image, because being sarcastic toward someone who's already in an aggressive mode will not help matters in the least; rather, it will elevate his hostility even more. Using bitter humor is like poison when trying to get cooperation from an angry person. The best of all solutions is to find some common ground where you both win, because no one ever actually wins in a fight. Even the so-called winner loses something. One of the most losing situations in my life is when I lose my witness which I have accomplished many times in my life, especially with my daughters; and I must say that those have been some of the most disappointing moments of my entire life.

Final Thoughts

Think about this for a moment: If we can't be in a good mood when alone, how are we going to feel and act when we're with a group of people? Have you considered how blessed you are? Are you in the habit of thanking the Lord daily for everything you have? Every morning when we wake up, before our feet hit the floor, we should say, "Good morning, Heavenly Father;" "Good morning, Jesus;" "Good morning, Holy Spirit," and thank them for another day. We should be thanking the Lord every day for the air that we breathe, the clothes on our backs, and the food in our homes. You can take a hundred people and have them write down their worst problem on a piece of paper and put them in a hat. Then, reach in, take one out, and trade your problem for theirs. I can just about guarantee that most, if not all, would say, "No, thank you. I will keep my own problem." Are you in the habit of praising and worshiping the Lord? What are your priorities? Are you still trying to council your friends? It would be a good idea to concentrate on bettering yourself and taking care of your own affairs before you talk to others about their issues. Until then, just be a good listener and pray for them.

Chapter Six

Change Your Perspective; Change Your Life

Who, me? Why is this one of the hardest things to do in life? Why is it that everyone would like for the world to change but resists the very thought of changing themselves? People do this, perhaps, because change may mean you need to stop living a certain way and start living this way, or stop talking a certain way, and start talking in a more positive, kind, and humble way. Change may mean you need to stop doing a few things and start doing some other things. Change may also mean you need to start thinking differently. Change is not easy. In fact, change is uncomfortable for most of us, but change is good. Although change may be one of the hardest things to accomplish, change is one of the most beneficial and profitable things that we ever could do. I must add a disclaimer, here, before we continue, because change for the better is what I'm talking about. Yes, it's possible to change in the wrong direction, and I'm sure that many people, including myself, have already made changes in that direction. The problem I had with change was, I didn't think I needed to change. I thought I was perfectly good just the way I was. My biggest thing with change is, learning what not to say as well as the timing on when to say a certain thing. I don't have this mastered, but I'm getting much better. So, what is it that needs to be changed in our lives? I'm sure that all of us could come up with several things. Change happens when an alteration comes about in our lives. Change means to leave something behind; and, for most of us, we don't want to leave the familiar because it's comfortable to us. I've heard many a sermon – and, more than likely, so have you, on how the Israelites wanted to go back to the land where they were slaves because it was familiar and comfortable to them. They were too blind to see that the Lord had their best interest at-heart. They feared change because change meant leaving the familiar, even though God had something better than anything they ever could have imagined. Unfortunately, they chose to wander in the desert. Life is a series of choices; and, from the time we become old enough to make our own choices, we become products of those choices. Yes we are products of the environment that we create for ourselves. There comes a point in time when we are accountable for all we say, do, and think; therefore, we are a product of our choices - nothing more and nothing less. Typically speaking, most of our life's symptoms are a direct result of our life's choices. I have made some very poor choices in my life; and, yes, I've made some changes that took me backwards in terms of love, joy, peace, and success in every area of my life. I have dated and fell in love with the wrong women at times, and have let others steal my joy and peace because I was lied to by the enemy to believe what they said or believed about me. One of the biggest and most important things that I've learned about choices is whatever you put before God is your God. That's my opinion, and I'm sticking to it. Putting other things before God is a losing proposition every time. Most of us have made gods from many things, to include money, sports and sports figures, movie stars, rock stars, job status, cars, men and women in our lives, and the list goes on. Please don't misunderstand. I'm not saying that we shouldn't enjoy those things, but we have our priorities mixed up when we can get excited about the things of the world and be so low-keyed about some of the more important aspects of living, like praising and worshiping the Lord Jesus and spending quality time with him. Most people won't even mention the name of Jesus in public or raise their hands and praise him. How can we not get excited and be in awe of the creator of the universe? I've asked myself this same question a time or two because there was a time in my life when I wasn't excited about Jesus. No one has or ever will reach perfection in any area of his or her life while here on earth. We all should view ourselves as a work in progress, not working toward perfection but learning how to view things from God's perspective. I believe that when we develop this perspective things work out. Life will not be without struggles, but will be much more peaceful, productive, and rewarding and will put us in a better position to achieve excellence and the blessings that the Lord has for us. Some people are of the opinion that God is not interested in every detail of their lives and that He's out to get them in some way. The Lord is alive and well, He cares about every detail in the lives of his children, and He's not out to get you. If he was out to get you, He could at any time. You can't hide from the Lord; He knows where you live. The main reason why the Lord is not out to get you is because He always operates out of love. It's totally out of God's character to want to harm you. Would you intentionally harm your child? I'm sure you would not. Now, this is not to say that the Lord doesn't chastise His children, because in Hebrews 12:6 the Lord reminds us that He disciplines those He loves, and in Proverbs 3:12 we are also reminded that the Lord disciplines those He loves, just as a father disciplines the son in whom he delights. So, when the Lord disciplines His children, He corrects out of love to direct us and put us back on the right path, and also to get our attention. It seems that many of us have re-created God into the image in which we want to visualize Him and that which is comfortable for us and fits in with our lifestyle. God wants us to view Him as the Holy God and His son as our Savior, our healer and helper in every area of our lives. God doesn't want us to view Him as a disinterested God who doesn't care about even the smallest and least important issues in our lives, because, to Him, everything in our lives is important. The Lord wants us to have life and have it in abundance, but that entails living life on His terms and not ours. I believe that when we change our perspective of God - from a distant God to a God who wants a walking, talking relationship with us, and strive to create that relationship with Him through Christ, he will reveal himself to us in ways that we never imagined, our lives will forever be changed, and we will never be the same again. You may see this next analogy more than once; it's worth repeating because when we talk about thinking like God, this is a key element. As in any relationship, communication is a two-way street. You must pray to God through Jesus Christ, and there is no other way. I know there are some people who, when they hear the word *pray*, get somewhat taken aback and think they don't know how to pray, or they say, "I don't pray; I meditate." That is so silly, and here's why: I'm going to use a love interest/relationship scenario, here, because I know most everyone can relate to it in some way. Let's say that you're a single person and you just saw the most amazing man or woman, whatever the case may be, in church, and you heard from a friend that he or she is interested in becoming better acquainted with you. If you never had communication with that person in terms of talking and exchanging conversation, how in the world do you ever expect to get acquainted with him or her? Oh, I know you're going to meditate on them, right? Do you see now how silly that is? Well, to be very honest with you, it's ignorant. You must talk to God through His son Jesus to have a relationship with Him, and it's impossible to have a meaningful relationship without doing this. It's your loss when you're not praying to the creator of the universe.

Let's change our perspective and just call praying talking to God, just like you would a friend. Have you ever opened up to a very close friend and shared some of the most troubling things in your life? Have you ever been to a counselor of any kind and had to share some very personal things? The same way you share with your friend or counselor is exactly the same way you share with God. Just talk to Him. Conversing with the Lord through the Holy Spirit is the best counseling anyone ever could have; but, first, there must be some communication on your part. If you went up to your friend and just stood there looking at him or her for hours, what kind of communication is that? If there is no communication, there is no relationship on which to base anything. Seek the Lord through the word of God, and bathe yourself in prayer. Then, you'll have a better understanding of God's perspective, and His wisdom will grow in you because true wisdom is viewing things from God's perspective. Also, you'll never know and understand the Lord's perspective if you aren't a born-again Christian who has the indwelling of the Holy Spirit and are reading His word and praying on a daily basis. Most people don't even say hello to God, let alone pray to Him. Is praying a fix all? Of course not; and there is no fix-all until the Lord returns or takes us home. Praying and reading the word of the living God, however, are the best arsenals we have, and who better to talk to than the creator of the universe?

"Our life's symptoms are typically a result of our life's choices."

Changing our perspectives is one of the best ways to overcome the obstacles and negative influences that come into our lives. Why is it that we view most of the obstacles that come our way as a hindrance? Yes, obstacles can be a hindrance or nuisance when they come into our lives; and, at times, they can be nothing short of heart-wrenching. Everything happens for a reason, though, and I don't believe there is such a thing as luck or happenstance. I believe most changes in life's directions are of Divine appointment. I moved to the Metro Atlanta, Georgia area from Iowa in 1994; and, two years prior to that move, it was very hard for me to make a living at anything I did. After much prayer and thought, the Lord prompted me to move to Atlanta. If the Lord had prospered me in Iowa I wouldn't have wanted to leave because business and life would have been great. This was God's way of closing the door on my life as I knew it in Iowa and taking me to a place where he wanted to plant me so I could grow to be the person He created me to be. Back then, when all of this was taking place, my perspective was, "What's going on? Why isn't anything working out for me? Why is business so bad?" Yes, I was moaning and groaning like most of us do; and there were many other things going through my mind at that time like fear and doubt. There were many times that I didn't know where my next dollar was coming from. There was no consistency whatsoever. My point is; God's purpose for my life started in Iowa, and He moved me to Georgia so He could begin to accomplish His true purpose in my life. Could the Lord have made it all happen for me in Iowa? Of course he could have. He could have made it happen for me in the desert if He so chose to, but God chose Georgia because there were people there whom He used as vessels. These people were instrumental in my healing and direction, and they helped guide me closer to the Lord's intended purpose for my life. Granted, there were some twists and turns along the way, mainly because of my choices and reluctance to change; and, as I look back at this time in my life, I can honestly say that I was not in complete obedience to the Lord.

"God cares about every detail of your life, and there isn't anything in your life that is insignificant to Him."

The Lord will never let tragedy or unpleasant things happen in your life without using the experience to teach you something, show you the good coming out of it, and to be glorified in the process. This is not a book about dating, but I would like to use this next illustration as another example of how the Lord uses people to direct our lives. I have used internet dating sites from time to time, although I have not dated many women at all from these sites. Over the years, however, while being single, I've met women once and then never seen them again. Throughout the dating process, I have met a few women whom I thought, "Yeah, I can hang out with her and see where this may go, but she wasn't interested in me in the least. Then, there were many women who were interested in me, but I wasn't interested in them. This really got me thinking. I started feeling inferior and thought to myself, "Am I not attractive and appealing to women anymore?" The fear and doubt was beginning to set in. Then, the Lord spoke to my spirit and told me to remove my profile from the dating sites, and that's just what I did. Under normal circumstances, the average man or woman would typically have found someone to date over a three-year period, but it's obvious the Lord had other plans for me; and, even at the time of this writing, I'm still not sure what that may be as far as a mate is concerned. The purpose of this example is to share that God had been turning the eyes and hearts of those women with whom I thought I could hang with. For whatever reasons, and those reasons aren't important, God didn't want me with any of these women. The correct perspective, here, is that God was protecting the two of us from something that was not in His best for either of us. During those times, I had been procrastinating with the more important things in my life, and one of them was the writing of this book. During the first two weeks of removing my profile from those dating sites, I wrote one complete chapter of this book, which was more than I had written in the previous six months. Dating is okay, and it has its place; but, if we're not careful, it can cause havoc in our lives, and it can steal our dreams if we let it. We let dating steal our dreams by putting more energy and emphasis on dating and finding that special someone than we do searching for God and trying to understand His will for our lives.

Most of the time, while growing up we have learned to see things from our parents' perspectives, from the perspective of people who were close to us, or from people who somehow were influential in our lives. Then, at some point in our lives, we come to a point where we think our parents and others who have had some influence on us are not that smart. We now have a mind of our own. Nobody can tell us what to do any more, and surely they can't have an influence on how we think or perceive life – we now have all the answers. We have the, "I'm a big boy/girl now," and "You're not the boss of me attitude." Sound familiar? Don't feel like the Lone Ranger, because I'm talking about me, too. Granted, some of our parents may have not been some of the best thinkers and role models, and they may have been messed up in their own ways, as well; however, I believe they had our best interests in mind. So, here we are – twenty, thirty, forty, fifty and older, our perspectives are just as skewed and narrow as ever, and it's not our parent's fault. So, how did our perspectives become so skewed and narrow? In my humble opinion, the one thing that has had a ton of influence in shaping our perspectives is the media, including the news, television programming, movies, sitcoms, and the list goes on. The media is a good thing to have; and yes, I'm grateful that we have such a thing. Throughout the years of my viewing the news, movies, and other media venues, I've been influenced to a point, just as most of the world has. In a sense, we all have allied ourselves with the gossip columnists, new media, and the many other avenues of print and video media out there. I'm very thankful for our media, and I believe we in the United States have the best media on the planet, and the most professional teams of men and women available to report and share the news with us. This discussion is not about the media, but how we sometimes choose to let any type of media shape our perspectives on life and the way it's supposed to be lived. This is all about our perspectives as individuals and – how we view life. I've made my next point in another section of this book. It's worth repeating, though, and you may see it repeated again several times over, because that's the crux of this book and the main point I want to get across. If you don't get anything else out of this book, please get this: Who knows more about life and the way to live life, than the one who created life? You got that right. No one! Yes, God knows more about the way to live, think, work, play, love, and give than anyone. With that being true, why is it that we have allied ourselves with everything else except the creator of the universe? We have looked everywhere and at everything except God for fulfillment and meaning in our lives. In order to be seekers of God, we must align ourselves with Him through His word. This is a must, if we want to tap into the true power of God. Be on your guard, however, because

- just as a car gets out of alignment after hitting pot holes - we can get out of alignment with God and the will of God as we go through the pot holes of life. That's a given. The pot holes of life can be anything from past and/or present personal relationships, habits and patterns of life that are at odds with the word of God, like, sex outside marriage, drug abuse, alcohol, anger, resentment, hostility, and unforgiveness. When we stay plugged into the word of the living God and bathe ourselves in prayer, though, it's less likely that that we'll fall for the lies and the trappings of the world – the pot holes of life.

"Sincere Christians align themselves with God and are seekers of God through prayer and the reading of His Word and are obedient to the Word."

Have I fallen for the lie before? Yes I have. I have based some decisions on what someone else has said they heard from the Lord. To protect their privacy, I'm not going to share in detail what that decision was, but I do want to talk about listening to God. Please, for your own good and the good of those you love, just because people tell you they heard from the Lord and they had a vision from the Lord about you, that doesn't make it so. I believe that if God gives someone a word about you, the Lord will give you some form of evidence of that word. In my situation, I knew in my own heart and spirit that I should not do what I was about to do; and for several months before I made that decision, I was hearing "no" in my spirit, but I did it anyway. And I did it for all the wrong reasons. I chose to make that decision, however, based on what someone else said, because I thought they may have been hearing something from God that I wasn't hearing. I thought they were more spiritual than I and were connected to God in a more powerful way because they had the gift of speaking in other tongues, and I didn't have that gift. In my experience, speaking in tongues has no bearing on whether you're connected to the Lord or not, and it has no bearing on your hearing from the Lord. Speaking in tongues has its place, and in no way am I suggesting that it's not a viable gift; however, I am suggesting that just because someone has been given the gift of speaking in tongues, that doesn't mean that he or she hears from God any better than you do if you don't speak in tongues. I don't believe our true friends will do anything on purpose to hurt us or to lead us astray. We must remember, though, that when someone gives us a word from the Lord, we must take it to the Lord in prayer and ask Him to reveal the truth about that particular thing. We need to be bold about our faith and our relationship with the Lord. We must know that He is always listening to us and wants to speak to us through His word and the Holy Spirit. Yes, God does speak to us through people and circumstances, but let's not set aside His word. I believe the reason most of us are not bold enough and have faith and believe that we can hear the truth from the Lord is because we know that we're not walking with the Lord as we should; therefore, because of our conscience, our faith is lacking in that area. When we are obedient to the Lord and His ways, there is no static or interference, and our conscience is at peace; therefore, we are in a better place to receive and hear from the Lord.

Final Thoughts

Change may call for removing and/or including things and/or people from our lives so that there's room , and with fewer distractions - for what God wants to add to our lives. We are a product of our choices - nothing more, and nothing less. Typically speaking, but not always, our life's experiences are a result of our life's choices. The Lord is interested in the smallest details of our lives, and He wants a walking, talking relationship with His children. How do you expect to get to know the Lord unless you spend quality time with Him through prayer and the reading of His word? When God closes a door, he's protecting you from something; and he always has something else for you, and that something is always better. Why let the world influence you, when you can be influenced by the creator of the universe - The Almighty God, Everlasting Father, and the Prince of Peace in Jesus Christ? The best way to get the most out of life is to align yourself with God and be seekers of God through prayer, the reading of His word, and being obedient to Him. When we're obedient to God, our conscience is in a better place for our faith to grow, hear, and receive, what He has for us. The Lord always has our best interests in mind, and He is not out to get you or harm you in any way. The Lord wants us to have abundance, but we must live life on His terms - not ours, to receive His abundance.

Chapter Seven

God Wants To Do a New Thing in You

Past successes don't always mean future success. Just because you had a great relationship with your girlfriend, spouse, friend, or business associate this year doesn't mean that your relationship will automatically be great next year. Those of you who are in business for yourselves know exactly what I'm talking about, because, in whatever you do, you must continually find ways to improve your business and the relationships that make that business survive. You must keep working at it. The success you had this year is no guarantee that success will automatically occur next year. In the same way, just because you had a great relationship with God this year doesn't guarantee that you will have a great relationship with Him next year. Just as we always must keep our relationships and businesses fresh, we need to look after and guard our relationship with the Lord even more. We must always work at keeping our relationship with the Lord fresh - unlike week-old bread - because the Lord wants to do a new thing in us, but we must allow Him to do so. As I recall my early years as a Christian, I hadn't a clue that the Lord wanted to do anything in me let alone do something new in me. I don't recall exactly what year this was, but I was involved in a holiday production at "Sunnyside Temple" the Church I attended. When it was over and the actors were greeting the audience members in the foyer, Dr. Polston, "my Pastor" came up to me and looked me in the eye and said – God is going to do something great in you one day. Has someone ever said something to you long ago that still resonates in your spirit? Well, this was one of those times for me, and I'll never forget it. At that time I was still hung up on things from my past and my self-esteem was way below par. The prophet Isaiah spoke this very thing in Isaiah: 18-19. He says, "Forget the former things; do not dwell on the past. See, I am doing a new thing! Now it springs up; do you not perceive it? I am making a way in the desert and streams in the wastelands." This is an expression of what the Lord was going to do for his people. This would surpass what He did for them in the past. Just as God wanted to do a new thing in His people back in the day of Isaiah, He wants to do a new thing in the lives of His children today, as well. The scriptures say God never changes, and that includes the true nature of the Lord in His character, His love and passion for His children, His desires to bless us, etc. At the same time, though, God is an ever-changing God when it comes to His relationship with His children and what He wants to do for them. He wants to bless you more today than He did yesterday. He wants to reveal more of Himself to you today than He did yesterday. The Lord is not stagnant. He's wants to move His children forward in the direction of His will so that we can be positioned to receive all that He has for us, but this takes cooperation and the willingness on our part. The Lord will never force His will upon us. The Bible also talks about losing our saltiness: "Salt is good, but if it loses its saltiness, how can it be made salty again. It is fit neither for the soil nor for the manure pile; it is thrown out" (Luke 14: 34-35). When salt loses its saltiness, it becomes a tasteless mass. For salt to lose its saltiness, it must be diluted with something, usually water or some other liquid. In the Biblical sense, this happens to Christians when we let the world influence us or dilute us. When Christians who are sold out on Christ let outside influences distract them and lead them away from what they know to be true, this is one of the major ways in which the danger of losing their saltiness comes in.

"God wants to do a new thing in us; but we must allow Him to do so, and we must be obedient."

We must be careful not to lose our flavor for the Lord. Just like the salt that has lost its flavor is not useful, we as children of God are of no use to Him if we lose our flavor. When we lose the saltiness that the Bible talks about, this basically means that we've lost our effectiveness for Christ in the world in which we live. When this happens, we no longer are good representatives for the Lord. So, in order for us to continue being effective for the Lord and to represent Him in a way that honors Him such that He truly deserves, we must keep our witness fresh and guard closely against losing our saltiness. Over the years, I have learned that the easiest way to lose our saltiness is to get involved with the world and think and behave like the world thinks. So, it makes sense to me that, in order to keep our witness fresh and not lose our saltiness and/or effectiveness for the Lord, we must guard against falling into a lifestyle of living and believing like the world lives and believes. I'm not saying that we shouldn't go out and enjoy ourselves with some good clean fun, but what I am talking about is a worldly lifestyle. You may say, "I read my Bible and pray every day." Praying and reading your Bible is of the utmost importance, but my experience has taught me that this is not enough.

"When we lose our saltiness, we lose our usefulness and effectiveness for God."

If you pray and read your Bible morning, noon, and night and are still caught up in the world, and letting the world influence you, you may already have lost your saltiness. Is this possible? Yes, because I've been there done that. We must make a conscious decision, as an act of our own will, to back away from the world and its ways that weaken our ability to witness for the Lord. We must protect ourselves from being diluted by the world's ways, which will lead to being complacent Christians. We also must be careful not to mix what we know to be true from scripture with other religious beliefs that are not of the Christian faith. If in fact you think you have already lost your saltiness you can get it all back if you really want to. Yes; once salt loses its flavor, it can never be used again; but thanks to the Lord and His great mercy and grace, He has a way for us to get our saltiness back. If we lose our saltiness, we can regain it by applying the word of God and prayer, and completely changing our thinking and behavior by aligning all our ways with the word of the living God in Christ Jesus. This is a deliberate act that we must engage in when seeking to regain our effectiveness and/or our usefulness for the Lord. Let's not use the grace of God as a safety net and take Him for granted, but rather as a tool to get back where we should be and to help others who have lost their usefulness and/or effectiveness for the Lord.

As mentioned earlier, reading the Bible and praying is of the utmost importance and is necessary in preventing us from sliding into a worldly lifestyle, as well as getting our effectiveness and/or usefulness back for the Lord. As mentioned in other chapters, we must bathe ourselves in prayer and the word of God. The words of

God will make you aware of the past, present, and future obstacles in your life and give you the best road map available for your life. We can't do anything about the wrong turns of our past; but, hopefully, we have learned from them. The Bible is life's light and road map and is one of the most precious assets available to you; and, along with prayer and obedience to the Lord, you can get through life and achieve anything if you put the Word to work for you.

There was a time in my life when I was a Sunday Christian. I would go to church on Sunday, and that was it. I would rarely read my Bible and, with the exception of praying over my meals, only pray to the Lord when I had a need in my life. Praying over meals is something I have always done after becoming a Christian, but consistently praying and reading my Bible had become very difficult for me. Why? I believe these very simple actions were difficult for me because the world still had a hold on me – my behavior, my attitude, my lifestyle, my thoughts, and the list goes on.

My soul was the Lord's; I knew who my God and Savior was; and I knew beyond a shadow of a doubt that if I was to leave this earth, I would be with Him. I was convicted in my spirit and felt weak at the knees after I did something that I knew was sin. I always found a way to defend my thoughts and behavior, even though they were tearing me up inside. I was, somehow, misaligned with the truth that the Lord had been trying to reveal to me. I tried so hard to choose to think and do the right things that were pleasing in God's sight, but I failed miserably. So, what was preventing me from getting into the word, praying, and living the abundant life that God called me to live? It was my past wounded-ness that was keeping me in bondage and, in turn, causing me to lose my saltiness and my excitement for the Lord. I surely thought I had forgiven others who have wronged me; and thought I had worked through other issues I had, as well, but

I was surely mistaken. Trying to get through these things on your own, apart from the healing power of the Lord Jesus is fruitless and only reaches the surface.

Some of you may never have heard of Prayer & Deliverance. I went through Prayer & Deliverance school several years ago, and it was one of the best things I have ever done for myself. I participated in the Sword of the Spirit Healing Ministries under Pastor Jack Valentino. This was a ten-month study once a week that completely changed my outlook on why I felt, talked, and behaved the way I did. I participated in the class three times, and continue to attend classes periodically. Here, with Pastor Jack's permission and blessing, I share with you the biblical basis for the Prayer and Deliverance Ministry: Christian healing does not come by making a broken thing good enough to work, but rather by delivering us from the power of that broken thing so that it can no longer rule us, and by teaching us to trust God's righteousness to shine in and through that very thing. The fundamental laws of God are written into the universe and affect all of our lives as surely as gravity. We all are subject to these laws, whether or not we believe them. When we transgress them, we set in motion forces that must be reaped by simple, impersonal law. Impersonal law is that which was created without bias. Gravity is such a law; no matter who jumps up, he or she will come down. These laws are absolute and eternal. In our sinful responses to wounding, we begin early to develop patterns of behavior that cause us to reap in adulthood - and sometimes before - those very things we hate and have judged in others. There are four basic laws, founded on the word of God, which has become the foundation of the entire discipline of Prayer Deliverance. The first law is honoring / dishonoring parents, in Deuteronomy 5:16; the second law is judging and becoming what you judge, in Matthew 7:1-

2 and Romans 2:1; the third law is sowing and reaping, in Galatians 6:7; and the fourth is forgiveness, in Matthew 6:12 and 14. This discipline also teaches that the most important thing to remember in the whole process is that God cannot do two things: He cannot override our will, and he cannot forgive in areas in which we have not forgiven. Thanks to Pastor Jack – a true vessel of the Lord – for being available as an instrument for the Lord's work in healing the wounded heart.

I also would like to share with you some of the things that were hindering me regarding the four basic laws founded on the word of God. The first is honoring / dishonoring my parents in conjunction with the sowing and reaping law. I have dishonored my parents in various ways from my early teens through my early twenties. There are many ways to disrespect parents. I have heard of many who have issues with forgiving a parent or a family member for hurting them. This can be very devastating in dating relationships as well as marriage. I thank and praise the Lord that my parents have always showed love and respect for each other and the people around them. I didn't think I had much difficulty with the issue of forgiveness or the lack thereof, but I surely did, and I have dishonored my parents through attitude and disobedience. I rebelled against their authority; and, in all reality, I must admit I was disrespectful. At that time of my life, I didn't think I was dishonoring them; but whether or not I thought I was does not matter. The fact is, I was disrespectful to my parents. So, I got married and had children of my own. I had three beautiful and wonderful daughters, who are now adults. At the time of this writing they are 24, 26, and 29 years old. I couldn't be more proud of the young women they have become. I love you girls more than you ever will know.

"Are you aware of the kind of seeds you planted with your parents that turned into bitter roots?"

Back in the day, when my children were younger, they would say things that would make me angry, and sometimes just down right indignant. Did I have any right to act that way? I sure didn't! I would get so upset at times that I would lose my cool and say things off the cuff that were hurtful to them. I was of the opinion that I was being disrespected by my own children, and that just tore me up inside. I expected more from my kids. They perceived that I was mean; but actually, I was very hurt and broken up inside and didn't know any other way to act but to react. For the longest time, I couldn't figure out why my kids talked to me the way they did.

I always have known of the sowing and reaping principal since the early days of my coming to know the Lord. Then, one day, the Lord spoke to my spirit very heavily. It was so strong that it could have been audible. The Lord told me that I have received from my children what I gave my parents. Simply put, I reaped the disrespect from my children that I sowed in the dishonoring of my parents. It was not their fault. It was just the principal of sowing and reaping that was taking place in my life. Just as it's impossible to plant soy beans and reap corn, it's also impossible to plant disrespect and reap respect. I have shared this principal in another chapter, and it's a principal that is not biased and was set by the Lord before He laid the foundation of the world. Today, I'm very proud to say that my daughters are grown women who love, honor, and respect their dad. I'm proud to call them my daughters. You girls are the BEST!!!

Secondly, the judging and unforgiving laws come into play together in my experience, and I don't wish to go into detail here because I want to respect the privacy of those involved. Yes, I have been hurt by several people over the years just as most people have been. Whether it was a divorce, a friendship, or a business arrangement doesn't matter. I was one of those people who thought that I could forget all about what transpired, and it would go away. Over time, however, the Lord showed me, through Prayer and Deliverance, that I couldn't make the effects of the hurt go away just by merely trying to forget about it and dealing with it on my own, apart from the power of the Holy Spirit and the living Lord in Christ Jesus.

The Lord also showed me that I had not forgiven the people who had hurt me; therefore, through my un-forgiveness, I was passing judgment on them, as well. No one has the power in and of themselves just to forget about the hurts of life and the scars they have caused. We can try to forget, but that's a waste of time and effort. Our heart and soul are what have been hurt, and this is the area in which the secular counseling arena falls short. In order for those inner areas to be healed, we must go to the only source that is able to touch and heal those areas, and that is the Almighty God, Everlasting Father, and Prince of Peace – Jesus Christ. There are no substitutes.

The Lord won't and can't make you forgive someone. Your forgiveness must be an act of your own will; and, with the help of the Holy Spirit, forgiveness can be achieved. Following are some other principals that I've learned from Pastor Jack and the Sword of The Spirit Healing Ministries. The habits, patterns, and structures are the fruit -- i.e. anger, rage, sabotage, fear, one bad relationship after another, always being the victim, negative expectations, etc. The root is ultimately judgment and un-forgiveness. The seed that is planted germinates from pain, fear and/or anger. Sins, judgments, and un-forgiveness need to be confessed, repented of, and washed by the Blood of Jesus Christ. We must put all structures, habits, and patterns to death on the cross; but, in order to take these things to the cross, we first must identify what they are and where they came from. In other words, we must identify their source. Then, and only then, can we take them to the Lord in prayer and ask Him to sever them at their roots. Thanks to Pastor Jack and the Sword of the Spirit Healing Ministries for allowing me to use this text.

"The Lord won't and can't make you forgive someone because forgiveness is giving up the right to be angry with that person."

I have also learned that we are not fixed once and for all. That's like saying we have eaten once and for all, and we never have to eat again. At the beginning of my Prayer & Deliverance class, I was really excited about the learning process. As the weeks went by, the excitement grew, and I was amazed at the things that I learned. I can't possibly share everything here that I learned, but I would like to share a few of the topics that were covered: Fruit to Root Patterns, Forgiveness, Bitter Roots, Honoring Father and Mother, Prenatal Wounds/Sins, Generational Sin, Inner Healing and Deliverance, Captive Spirit, and many others. I highly recommend that anyone seek out Prayer & Deliverance as a way of dealing with past hurts.

If we continue on the same path, without getting down to the truth of where our problems and issues began, we will continue to go through the same issues day after day, week after week, month after month and year after year. If you think, for one minute, that deep spiritual issues can be healed through a secular counselor or by yourself, you may just be in for a long life of being in and out of relationships, as well as acting out your past hurts on the loved ones and people all around you. A secular counselor does not know how to deal with the topics that I mentioned above; and neither do you, unless you were trained in those areas. You just can't think and reason them away. Secular counselors have their place and are valued professionals, but they are not trained in dealing with spiritual issues. Secular counselors are not going to take their findings to the cross and pray with you. That's the only way to heal spiritual issues, and it's impossible to heal them without the power of the Holy Spirit. With the guidance of the Holy Spirit, it's the Prayer Deliverance Minister's job to identify the bitter roots and take them to the throne of God through prayer; this is where the healing begins.

What I've learned from my dear friend Pastor Jack has changed my life and will continue to affect me as long as I live. Prayer Deliverance is not a fix-all, as nothing really is. We will experience the true fix-all when we go home to be with the Lord, but the Prayer and Deliverance ministry is one of the best starting points that I know of. It's an on-going process that needs to be practiced daily. Have I been healed of some things that will never return? Yes. Are there things that try to come back to taunt me? Of course there are. I have an advantage now, though. Through Prayer & Deliverance, the Lord has put it in my spirit the ability to recognize those ugly things when they try to work their way back into my life. The Lord reveals to me that they are lies from the enemy and are there to harm me, and He also brings to my attention where these feelings, attitudes, habits, and patterns came from. The Lord has armed us with the best healing and battle tools on the planet – the Holy Spirit, Prayer, and the Word of God. Keep your eyes on Him. The Lord is still the great healer and physician; He is the Almighty God, the Everlasting Father, and the Prince of Peace. To Him shall be all Glory, Honor, and Praise.

Final Thoughts

Are you counting on your past success to propel you through to the next year or next level? We must not take our past successes for granted, but continue to strive not for perfection, but excellence.

In order for advancements to take place, there must be new growth, new discoveries, and new visions. We always must keep our witness fresh, unlike week-old bread. We must always strive for a closer and more intimate walk with the Lord in order to protect ourselves from losing our saltiness. We must be careful not to let the world taint us with its views and beliefs; otherwise, we lose our usefulness for God. God wants to do a new thing in us, but we must allow Him to do so. Remember not to mix the truth that you know from the word of God with the world's views and other views that are not of the Christian faith. The word of God is life's best road map; it's the light that keeps you from stumbling. Let the Bible be your GPS. Where are you in reference to honoring and dishonoring your parents? If your parents aren't around anymore, you can still take the issues to the Lord and share whatever grievances you may have, and receive peace, healing, and forgiveness. What kinds of seeds have you planted in your relationship with your parents? Have you truly forgiven your parents and others for the offenses that you believe they have brought upon you? Do you know why you act as you do and say the things you say? Do you know what triggers your behavior? The Lord can't and won't make you forgive someone; it must be an act of your own will. Forgiveness means giving up your right to be angry with that person. Please remember that secular counselors have their place, but they are not trained in working with and identifying deep spiritual issues that involve the spirit and the dark forces that we struggle against, which are trying to destroy our love, hope, and joy.

Chapter Eight

Eight Deadly Sins That Leave No Room for God

Far too many Christians are seeing God and life through their flesh and not with the Spirit that is available to them. Is that possible? Yes. I used to be one of them; and, every now and then, the enemy tries to instill those crippling thoughts. When we view God and life with our flesh, there is no room for God; and, if there is no room for God, then there is no room for fellowship with Him and no room to receive the blessings He wants to give us. I had experiences with all of these next topics at various times in my Christian walk as well as before I became a Christian. It's humbling to share them; but, if I can touch one person, it's all worth it. I call them the eight deadly sins that leave no room for God; they are Pride, Greed, Lust, Envy, Gluttony, Sloth, Anger, and Unbelief. When we live our lives with any of these deadly sins playing an active role in our lives, it's next to impossible for us to open the eyes of our heart so that God can fill our lives with what He wants, which is for us to fill our lives with Him. With God, though, all things are possible (Matthew 19:26).

Pride says, "Hey, look at me!"

Pride – We all have had problems with pride, in some form or fashion, at some point in our lives; and, even if we think we've dealt with it, sometimes pride has a tendency to want to creep back in. We have discussed pride in a previous chapter, but we will be discussing a somewhat overlooked area of pride. The kind of pride that we're talking about, here, is the pride of self-righteousness. Have you ever known people who always are willing to tell you how good they are, how much they pray, how much they read the Bible, and how obedient they are? I have had someone tell me that they're following God 100%. The moment I heard that statement I wanted to say something, but I did not. No one follows the Lord 100%. Remember what Jesus told the rich man? "Go sell everything you have and give it to the poor." We must be careful of thinking too highly of ourselves; because, more times than not, this type of thinking is a good indication of self-righteousness. If, in fact, this type of sharing is not shared with the right intentions, this is dangerously close to haughty pride, and haughty pride is wicked.

We must be aware of our true intentions and honestly identify our motives when sharing, and especially when sharing spiritual things. I have learned to go to the Lord in prayer and ask Him to bring to my attention the prideful habits and patterns that hinder me. I also would like to point out that the issue of self-righteousness applies to the non-Christian community, as well, because when people say that they don't need to be born-again to be with the Lord when they die, what they are saying is, "I don't need to claim the death on the cross to be saved." I'm not buying into all that they say. In essence, they have become their own god; and, of course, they think this way because that's the common response for the carnal-minded person. Spiritual-minded people, people who are filled with the Holy Spirit, are fully aware of how much they need Christ because they believe that Christ died on the cross for their sin and the world's sin. They believe that whosoever believes in Him shall have eternal life. Psalm 10:4 says; "In his pride the wicked does not seek him; in all his thoughts there is no room for God". This is one concept that I had a problem with, and I recall when the Lord brought this to my attention. At first, I said, "No way; not me. I'm not that way." At least I didn't think I was. I don't want to believe that most Christians who really love the Lord have this type of pride knowingly, because I didn't - knowingly, that is. I fought the Lord for a long time on this one, and I'm glad to say that He won. At the time when I gave in and released my pride to the Lord it was as if something pierced my heart. In the beginning, I was hurt and embarrassed because I had been found out. Typically, that's the first response for most of us because the awareness really sets in when we've been found out. We don't want anyone to know about the dirty stuff on us, now do we? Granted, if someone asks you about your walk and your relationship with the Lord, by all means go ahead and share. Please do yourself a favor, though: Don't pride yourself on how good you are, and don't beat yourself up with how bad you are, either. The Lord says that all of our righteousness is as filthy rags. That means that, even in our best behavior, the Lord is not impressed; so, let's not be impressed with ourselves, either. When we hold ourselves in such high esteem, this type of pride is a form of self-worship. Many of us choose not to associate pride with our Church-going family, but it exists there, as well. Church can become a self-setting trap for pastors and members. Romans 12:3 says; "For by the grace given me, I say to every one of you; do not think of yourselves more highly than you ought, but rather think of yourselves with sober judgment, in accordance with the measure of faith God has given you." Here's another example of what I'm talking about.

Have you ever held conversations with people, and - from the very onset - the conversations were all about them, and the only thing they talked about was their selves? You learned everything about them without their ever asking you how you are and what's going on in your life. I have been at gatherings before and witnessed this kind of behavior first-hand. If this is you, please take it down a few notches and re-think. With an attitude such as this, it's very difficult to open your heart to make room for God. This type of pride can also hinder people from accepting Christ as their personal Savior. We all need to know that life is not all about us. Life is all about God; and, with God, all things are possible (Matthew 19:26).

Greed – "I want it when I want it, and I'll do anything to get it."

Greed - another area that hinders the presence of the Lord. As I mentioned in an earlier chapter, my dad was one of the most giving persons I ever have known in my life. I grew up learning how to give - not just monetarily, but giving of myself, as well. As I said before, most of my life - before my dad became a Christian - I had witnessed my dad showing more love for his fellow man than I had witnessed among any Christian I ever had known during my Christian life. Even up to the very day of this writing, I haven't seen from anyone the kind of giving I saw in my dad. My dad was the most selfless man I ever have known. That's just how the Lord wired him. I grew up with this kind of mentality; so, when I see or hear of people displaying greed, it's troubling to me. Greed comes in many different forms, and most of us have experienced it to some extent in our lives. I recall the 1987 movie *Wall Street* with Michael Douglas, as he portrayed the character Gordon Gekko. The character says that greed is good – greed works. *Wall Street* was put together very well and was indeed a good movie; however, I must disagree with the critics that, although greed appears to work well in the movie for a short time, the characters paid dearly for it in the end. According to the Lord, greed just doesn't work well in real life. According to Miriam Webster; greed is the selfish and excessive desire for more of something than is needed. This topic of greed can go in many directions, but the concept I want to discuss here comes from the two key words in Webster's definition – *selfish* and *excessive*. As in any endeavor in life, the person who pursues something with a selfish mindset is going after it for the wrong reasons. Likewise, when we go after something in an excessive manner, we lose focus on the more valuable things in life and end up neglecting them. Please don't misunderstand me, here. I'm not saying don't go after your goals with all you've got; when you do, though, please don't lose sight of doing whatever it is that you're doing for the right reasons. The right reasons are different for everyone and are rarely the same for anyone. When selfishness and excessiveness are involved in any pursuit, there may be disaster waiting in the wings. We can always take everything we do back to the seed principal. We will reap what we sow. Being self-serving never does anyone any good. W. Beran Wolfe, M.D., was a psychiatrist and author who said if you live only for yourself, you are always in immediate danger of being bored to death with the repetition of your own views and interests. Thought provoking, isn't it? No one has learned the meaning of life until he has surrendered his ego to the service of his fellow men. The Lord tells us, in James 3:16, "For where you have envy and selfish ambition, there you find disorder and every evil practice." Just as the Lord says that you can identify a tree by its fruit, in the same way, you can identify the wisdom in people by the way they talk and act. Do we talk and act in a way that reflects an attitude of, "I matter most; what I think is more important; and are our mouths and thoughts as foul as dung?" Using foul language is as self-serving as we can be. What good does it do to curse? What good does it do to say those four-letter words? Just think about it: It does no one any good at all, – not even to you. The only thing it does is serve your old evil nature, which has been building inside of you over the years, and wants to reveal itself from time to time. You need to get rid of that garbage and start planting the kinds of seeds that, when matured, will reap you bountiful rewards in this life and the next. In order to change the fruit, the old tree must be severed at its root and a new seed must be planted. If you're not saved, the first seed that needs to be planted is being born-again into the family of God by accepting Christ as your personal savior. If you are a born-again believer, the bottom line is, you need to start acting and talking like a King's kid. I have heard people say, "I like to say the F word." Again, that is self-serving at its best; you're saying it to please yourself, and it helps no one. In my humble opinion, if you can't find a better word to say than the F word, keep your mouth shut.

Excessiveness - Miriam Webster terms excessiveness as an amount or degree too great to be reasonable or acceptable. When someone wants something so bad that it's unreasonable or unacceptable, that's where the problem lies; because when people want things too badly, most of the time they are willing to do some things that they wouldn't normally do, like lie, cheat, steal, put their goals before their family and morals, forget about God in everything, and the list goes on. We should not compromise our beliefs or morals to achieve success. There's nothing wrong with wanting to be successful and to have more than we actually need. The Lord says; "The thief comes only to kill, and steal and destroy. I (the Lord) came that they may have life and have it more abundantly (John 10:10). The problem is not in wanting more. The problem lies in the lengths people are willing to take to achieve that desired goal. Is your desire so strong that everything else takes a back seat? Does achieving that goal have you mesmerized? Does wanting that certain man or woman in your life have your mind so messed up that you are willing to do anything to win his or her love? Look, I could go on and on, here, but I believe you're getting the idea. The bottom line, here, is to not go to such exaggerated lengths to achieve something – including a love interest, that you forget about the Lord and His ways. When you put other things before the Lord, you set yourself up to be exploited by sin, and you degrade yourself in many ways. You pay the price to pay for acting in such a way; and, believe me, you don't want to pay the price.

"Lust will hurt you more than you know."

Lust – The dictionary terms lust as an overwhelming desire, or craving, or an unrestrained sexual craving; however, the Bible talks about lust in an entirely different way. Matthew 5:28 says, "But I tell you that anyone who looks at a woman lustfully has already committed adultery in his heart. Are sinful acts more dangerous than sinful thoughts? Of course they are. The Lord is warning us that if these desires are left without the belief that they are sinful and wrong in His eyes and need correction, then more dangerous and sinful acts will occur. Now, don't get me wrong; I'm not saying that it's ok to look at a woman with lust. What I am saying is that you do not want to have the mentality that says, "If I have already committed the sin just by looking, I may as well go ahead and commit the physical act." No, no, of course you shouldn't!

There are many other consequences that go with the physical act that are not associated with just looking. Just to name a few, how about losing your witness, creating a soul tie, contracting disease, becoming pregnant, developing hurtful emotions and feelings; and, yes, we must mention fornication and adultery. Have I committed a sexual sin in my past? Yes, I have. I'm not proud of it, and I have paid dearly for it. I share this with you to let you know that I have messed up, as well. I don't walk around thinking I'm "holier than thou;" and, surely, I don't think I'm better than anyone. I'm writing this book because I have messed up terribly and have experienced most - if not everything—that I write about; and, if I can help some of my readers - and hopefully all of them - then I have been successful at what the Lord has commissioned me to do.

The most important thing, here, is that we must be careful not to break fellowship with the Lord. Secondly, we must take care of our bodies. 1 Thessalonians 4:3–8 (NIV) says, "It is God's will that you should be sanctified: that you should avoid sexual immorality; that each of you should learn to control his own body in a way that is holy and honorable, not in passionate lust like the heathen who do not know God." 1 Thessalonians 4:7-8 says, "For God did not call us to be impure but to live a holy life. Therefore, he who rejects this instruction does not reject man but God." The standards for living during biblical times were not very respectable in reference to sex; and, in my opinion the standards of the world in which we live today are not any better. Our goal as Christians who are followers of Christ, should be to become more like Christ in our day-to-day activities at home, work, and play. The Lord wants to give us more than even we want, but he can't because of the condition of our hearts. Let's live in accordance with the Lord and be in total obedience to Him, then watch the miracles come into our lives and be forever changed.

Envy – Envy is defined as the feeling of displeasure when hearing about the success of someone other than you. Proverbs 23:17 says, "Do not let your heart envy sinners, but always be zealous for the fear of the Lord." Have you ever been displeased when someone you know has achieved a level of success for which you hoped, but which has not been in the cards for you? It could be money, a job, successful career, or being happily married. Envy goes hand-in-hand with lust and is lust working at its best. When we lust, envy is sure to follow; and, if we already are in the process of envy, then we have been lusting for quite some time - only God knows how long. Proverbs 14:30 says, "A heart of peace gives life to the body, but envy rots the bones." I believe the Lord is saying that where there is envy there is no peace, and that envy can make your body sick, as well. A person's low self-esteem can breed envy. This can happen when people compare themselves with others and, in their own eyes, they pale in comparison. In turn, they put themselves down; this results in low self-esteem, which results in envy.

Have you ever known people who look great in photographs, yet they say they hate their pictures? As a photographer, I have seen this behavior expressed in men and women for many years. This mentality comes from poor self-esteem and typically stems from being beaten down verbally and not being loved properly, with positive affirmation, in their younger years. Aristotle defined envy as the pain caused by the good fortune of others. It's very unhealthy for someone to be unhappy when someone else succeeds. We should always think the opposite when someone succeeds. This is important for two simple reasons: First, people who have been blessed in some fashion or another have had their lives enhanced and turned upside down with good fortune. Evidently, they have had their socks blessed off because of the blessing that God has bestowed upon them. It doesn't matter what the good fortune was. The fact is, this fortune impacted their lives in a positive way. It just doesn't make any sense not to rejoice with someone because of envy. This blessing has made someone very happy. We should be happy for them and with them.

The second reason we should be happy for other's blessings is that we should have the faith and action reflected in our words and behavior that says, "Wow! That's great that the Lord blessed them; because, if God blessed them, then God can bless me, too. If God did it for them, God can and will do it for me." You see the difference? Life is way too short to get hung up on the mentality of "Why them?" and "Why not me?" Just be patient; and, if you're doing what you're supposed to be doing in terms of your relationship with the Lord, your time will come. God promises that. Deuteronomy 8:18 says, "But remember the Lord your God, for it is he who gives you the ability to produce wealth." Please know that the word wealth doesn't always pertain to money and finances. The word wealth is not only speaking of financial wealth, but also a healthy relationship or marriage, love, peace, joy – you know, all the fruits of the Spirit.

How many sick people are there in the world whose bodies need some type of healing miracle? One of the greatest gifts of wealth anyone ever could have is to be healed of a disease. If you had cancer, would you want a million dollars or would you want to be healed? We all know what the answer to that question is, but it's a great example that gets the point across. Sometimes, we Christians fall to envy because we see people being successful and blessed in the world, and people still getting ahead in life with no responsibility to obey the Laws of God. Please know that, for a time, it may appear that they are getting ahead and prospering, but I guarantee you that the Lord will have His say in their lives at some point in time.

The Bible says that the Lord is slow to anger. He gives his children - those who have accepted His son Jesus as their personal savior - and those who are not his children - those who have not accepted His son as their personal savior - time to repent, walk obediently, and/or accept Jesus as their personal savior. The Lord blesses us accordingly, and those blessings vary in the form in which they come. The Bible tells us, in Matthew 5:45, that the Lord rains on the just and the unjust. God chooses the blessing and the person whom He's going to bless. So, if the Lord chooses to bless someone, who are we to go against the Lord and not be happy for that person's blessing? God wanted to bless him or her, so let's rejoice in this blessing, as well. If we are bothered because we think those who receive God's blessings aren't Christians – not following the Lord as the Bible teaches us to do, then that's the Lord's business and He will deal with those persons in His own way and in His own time, not ours.

Gluttony - Gluttony is not universally considered a sin by the world's standards, but let's not let the world be our life's GPS. Christians should let the word of God – not the world - be their GPS and the light that shines and lights their way to discern right from wrong. I have lived in the world long enough to know that living outside of the will of God is not the place to be; it's dangerous, at best, and it's not even second best. Gluttony is typically known as over consumption of food and drink in excess, to the point of waste. There's nothing wrong with getting your fill with a good meal. I must get that out of the way before we continue. I also must state that I mean no disrespect to the many people who are over-weight need to shed some pounds. This is not about you and your weight, but about the sin of gluttony that thin people are guilty of, as well. I'm guilty of gluttony, too, and eating has been a struggle for me most of my adult life. So, as with all the subjects of this book, if I'm talking about anyone, it's me. For me, gluttony is not just about over-eating to the point of waste, but thinking about what my next meal is going to be, even before finishing the one I'm eating. Now, I don't think like that anymore, but my thoughts have gone there before. I was raised around eating tons of food. In my Eastern European, culture - when family members would visit each other - cousins, aunts, uncles, and so on - one of the first things I recall them asking is, "Did you eat?" and "Are you hungry?" then saying, "C'mon, sit; eat." Also, if you just ate a small plate they would say, "C'mon; eat some more. You hardly ate anything," and they would fill your plate for you again. My relatives around the country reading this will be laughing,- knowing exactly what I'm talking about because they have all experienced this, as well. I must say that they definitely didn't mean any harm and always had good intentions. It was just a way of life for my family. When someone came over to our homes, it was our custom to serve them.

Proverbs 23:20 says, "Do not join those who drink too much wine or gorge themselves on meat, for drunkards and gluttons become poor and drowsiness clothes them in rags." Also the health benefits of over-eating are unhealthy, as well. Our country has become one of the unhealthiest places on earth because of our eating habits. It seems like most of us live to eat instead of eating to live. Going back to earlier chapters on thinking and renewing your mind, the same applies here when it comes to eating. We all need to re-train our thinking when it comes to eating; doing so will be good for the mind and body.

Sloth – There are several terms for sloth/slothfulness; just a few such terms are slow, lazy, and slumber. I must admit that I just had a slothful morning, and I mention that because – during the evening of this writing - I recall my attitude and thoughts being slothful. I'm rarely ever that way. Why was I slothful? I woke up that way. When I woke up, there was something very different about my countenance. I couldn't place it; I just wasn't my normal self. Typically, when I wake up – and before I get out of bed - I routinely say, "Good morning, Heavenly Father; Good morning, Jesus; and Good morning, Holy Spirit. Thank you for another day." Then, I begin to pray before I get out of bed. That didn't happen on this particular morning. I had stayed up very late the night before and didn't read my Bible and pray as I typically do. In my experience – both on this particular morning and in the other instances of my life where slothfulness reared its head - I believe it's because I did not call on the power of the Lord and His Holy Spirit to revive me. I typically do this every morning. I have noticed that when I start and end my day with the Lord, I feel more energized and full-of-life the following day. I liken this to starting my day with a healthy breakfast to prepare my body for the day and eating healthy nutritious meals throughout the day to keep me energized throughout the day. Likewise, just as the body needs its fuel, our spirit needs to be fed with prayer, praise, worship, and the Bible – the word of God. Just like a car won't run at its peak when there's water in the fuel mixture, our bodies and spirits won't function at their highest peaks with the junk of the world being administered to them. In particular, the body and spirit need the word of God because they crave it. If you truly have the Holy Spirit living inside you and you're not getting fed with the word of God on a regular basis, the power of the Holy Spirit is limited in your life – and much of the time you will feel slothful – and then you'll wonder why. This topic was discussed in another chapter so we won't be discussing it here, but I do want to point it out because it's worth repeating: If you're not spending quality time reading the Bible, you're cheating yourself of one of the most precious gifts that you ever could receive. The Word of God and time spent with God are priceless and the best thing you ever could give yourself.

Anger - I must admit that I had an anger problem in my past, and I always thought I had a good excuse for it. My concern was, "They pressed my buttons. They knew what they said or did would tick me off, so why did they say it? Why did they do that? If they hadn't done or said *that*, I wouldn't have reacted the way I did." That sounds like a great excuse, now, doesn't it? I was good at justifying my behavior and was very wrong for doing so. As I now look back on my life as a child and pre-teen, I understand where that anger came from. When I met Pastor Jack, of "Sword of the Spirit Healing Ministries," I learned much about where these emotions came from. I can only recall my father getting upset in our home once when I was a child. He was the peacemaker, and my mom – bless her soul - was a little firecracker. I don't want to label my mother an abuser because she wasn't, but she wasn't afraid to discipline me if she felt I deserved it. I believe I was hurt outside of my immediate home. From the age of eight until about fifteen, I recall watching my uncles argue with each other and then start fist-fighting and rolling on the ground. This was a regular event at these types of gatherings, because my uncles would get drunk and verbally abuse each other. I also recall one of my uncles grabbing my ear, pulling it very hard as he was walking me across the street, and kicking my rear as we were walking. Yeah, right! Boy did that hurt. I remember hearing one of my uncles say kids are to be seen and not heard. I didn't think anything about that statement then. Now, I know that what he said is one of the cruelest things anyone could ever say to a child. I was always around their arguing and bickering, and I watched the arguing and bickering escalate into a raging event. I do want to point out that this did not take place in the home where I grew up, but at family events outside the home. Yes, it's possible to get programmed into certain behaviors when growing up; but, then, there comes a time when we must discern for ourselves what behaviors are acceptable, unacceptable, and - most of all - healthy. No matter where the anger comes from, we are all morally responsible for the choices that we make. It's time to stop playing the blame game and to stop singing the "Somebody done me wrong" song. The Lord says, in James 1:19-21, "My dear brothers, take note of this; everyone should be quick to listen, slow to speak, and slow to become angry. Therefore, get rid of all moral filth and the evil that is so prevalent and humbly accept the word planted in you, which can save you." As I shared in a previous chapter, I'm not a counselor or a theologian; and I really don't like to give personal advice. In all fairness, though, I must tell you that if you have an anger problem you better find someone who can help you identify where that anger came from and take it to the throne of God. If you don't, it will, more than likely, create havoc in your life and wreck whatever life you may have left. I believe that anger is a learned behavior, and there may be spiritual issues from way back when to deal with as well.

I highly recommend seeking a trained individual who knows about these kinds of issues: mainly a Prayer Deliverance Minister. They are Christian professionals who are trained to identify these hidden spiritual issues of life that hinder us from living a bondage-free life. Yes, we are free from the bondage of sin because of whose we are through Christ: We are His children. Many people think that we can send blanket prayers to God, and that's all we need. I believe we need to be specific about the certain areas of our lives that have been a hindrance to our wellbeing. We must first identify the causes of our feelings and the whys of our behavior's. Then, we must bring them out of the darkness into the light of Christ, ask Him to sever them at their roots, then walk free. Everything must be brought to the throne of God through the cross of Christ – that's where the healing is. If you're interested in learning more about the Prayer Deliverance ministry, by all means, please take a peek at Pastor Jack's website at: soshealingministries.org.

Unbelief – In my opinion, this is by far the greatest sin that any of us ever could do. Specifically, I'm talking about doubting God and His word, and not believing that Christ is who he says he is. This is the most dangerous thing that anyone ever could do. Over the years, I have heard many sermons on the sin of Adam and Eve and always have heard that the sin was disobeying God and eating from the tree of the knowledge of good and evil. Yes, disobeying God is sin; however, I don't believe that was the *first* sin in the garden. I believe the first sin was in *not* believing in the word of God. God gave His word, and Satan impressed upon Man that the word of God was not true and that we don't have to obey it. Satan also convinced Man that there would be no punishment for disobeying the word of God. At that point in time, Satan's main objective was to make God a liar and to convince Man that God would not do what He says He would do. Satan is still up to the same trickery today, trying to instill in people that the word of God is a lie.

Satan still uses people to try and discredit God and His word. As mentioned in an earlier chapter, it's mainly those of the New-Age movement and their spiritual beliefs that are leading the way in this attack against the Bible. They teach that there is no such thing as sin, there is no hell, and everyone is going to go to heaven. They believe that everyone has a unique way to get to heaven and that Christ is not the only way. That's blasphemy at its best!

These people also teach that the Bible is man's idea and is not the word of God without error. I recall conversations that I have had with people who don't claim to be Christians and have been involved in New Age Studies. One of my questions was, "If there are other ways to have your sins forgiven and to get to heaven, why did Christ die on the cross?" Their answer was, "I don't know." I responded with, "Don't you think that an event like that is important enough to look in to?" I didn't get an answer. I also asked, when Christ says that I am the way the truth and the life, no one can come unto the Father except by me, what – if anything - does that mean to you?" I never have received a good, concrete answer from anyone.

When Christians have unbelief, it's not that they don't believe that Christ is their personal Savior; they believe this. Christians are not hidden from the problems of life and the lies of the enemy. Satan will always try to get everyone to disbelieve in the things of the Lord. In fact, the Lord says that we are going to have trials and tribulations, and the world is going to hate us because we love Him. Jesus said, in John 15:18-19, "If the world hates you, keep in mind that it hated me first. If you belonged to the world, it would love you as its own. As it is, you do not belong to the world, but I have chosen you out of the world. That is why the world hates you." When this happens, we sometimes begin to fret, then our unbelief raises its ugly head.

Unbelief also tries to squeeze its way into our minds when we get blindsided with life: loss of job, health issues, bills, and the list goes on. When we come up against these tough times; this is where faith and trust come in. The Lord wants us to hold tight to his promises in scripture. In Philippians 4:19, the Lord promises, "My God will supply all your needs according to his riches in Christ Jesus." The Lord also tells us, in Matthew 6:25 & 27, "Therefore I tell you, do not worry about your life, what you will eat or drink; or about your body, what you will wear. Is not life more important than food and the body more important than clothes? (27) Who of you by worrying can add a single hour to his life?" Then, in Mark 6:33-34, the Lord tells us how to receive: "But seek first the kingdom and his righteousness, and all these things will be given to you as well. Therefore do not worry about tomorrow, for tomorrow will worry about itself. Each day has enough trouble of its own." I believe that seeking the kingdom and his righteousness involves bathing ourselves in the word of God by meditating and memorizing the word of God, attending worship services regularly, praising and worshiping Him, and obedience to the Lord and His word. If we are missing any of these life-giving links, we may not be seeking the Lord with all our heart, mind, and soul, therefore, missing God's best.

Final Thoughts

How are you seeing God? Do you see Him with your flesh or with the Holy Spirit that's in you? The unsaved can't view God with the Spirit because they do not have the Spirit of God residing in them. Do you pride yourself with how good you are, and do you brag about how closely you walk with the Lord? It's great to feel good about whose we are in Christ, but we all must be careful of falling into the mode of self-righteousness. The Pharisees were self-righteous, and the Lord was very displeased with them. Greed does not work in the long run, and greed is never any good. Anything done with selfish motives is not true success, because it's done with only you in mind. Whether it's lust for a tangible object or for the opposite sex - unless you're married and it's for your spouse, lust, in any form is not good.

Losing your witness is always at stake when lust is a choice. Are you bothered when someone succeeds and you don't? If so, envy is trying to work its way into your life. If the Lord brought success to someone, he could just as easily bring it to you, too; so, be happy for others when they are successful. Success may be in store for you next. Let's not let the world be our road map for life; rather, let's let the word of God be our GPS. Just as we need to start our day with a nutritious meal, it's equally important - if not more important - to begin and end your day with the Lord. When we do this, we are, in essence, asking God to be part of our every day and night. Do you want this from the Lord? Seeking the kingdom and his righteousness involves bathing ourselves in the word of God by meditating and memorizing the word of God, attending worship services regularly, praising and worshiping Him, and obedience to the Lord and His word. If we are missing any of these life-giving links, we may not be seeking the Lord with all our heart, mind, and soul, therefore, missing God's best. If you're not a born-again believer who believes that Christ is the only way to be with the Heavenly Father when we leave this earth, I would find people who are believers and have them share their faith with you; and please, ask God to open your heart and reveal the truth to you. We, as Christians, must trust the Lord for all of our needs and not worry about tomorrow. The Lord knows exactly what our needs are, and He promises his children He will supply them. We also must remember to seek God on a daily basis, pray, read the word, memorize the word, and praise and worship the Lord. Doing these things will bless you more than you ever could imagine. Do you believe that Jesus is the only way, or do you believe like the other religions of the world that you have your own way to be with God when your soul leaves your body? Is Jesus a liar or is He telling the truth? You must choose then reap the corresponding rewards.

Chapter Nine

God's Wisdom is
Life's Ultimate GPS

As with any venture in life, and especially in writing this book, the wisdom of God was a must; and there was no way I ever could have accomplished this task without His divine guidance. Like many of the men and women from the bible - Apostle Paul, King David, King Solomon, Joseph, Hanna, Ruth, Deborah, and the list goes on, I had to rely on the wisdom of the Lord, and in no way could I have accomplished what the Lord had commissioned me to do had I not relied on and followed the wisdom of God. Of course, all the people I mentioned above had their own issues and sin to deal with, but they were truly sold out on God. These men and women knew that the Lord was their source for everything. In this chapter, it's only fitting to set our main focus on the book of Proverbs and King Solomon's life, because - except for Christ - he was the wisest man who ever lived. I want to lay the foundation for this chapter by introducing Solomon and the book of Proverbs.

Solomon penned the majority of Proverbs with help from Agur and Lemuel, who contributed to some of the latter chapters. If you want to learn how the wisdom of the Lord thinks and behaves, read the book of Proverbs. I recall many years ago as a new believer, when asking Dr. Polston "my first Pastor" how do I know when it's God I'm hearing? How do I know when it's the correct decision? I'll never forget his answer without hesitation. Dr. Polston said read Proverbs and God will speak to you and reveal His wisdom to you. I only wish I would have had some common sense at that time to know what the consequences were for not being obedient to God and what He was trying to teach me through Proverbs. Yes, I have learned the hard way, but you surely don't have to. One of the greatest and simplest displays of the Lord's wisdom in the life of Solomon was when two prostitutes were claiming to be the mother of the same child. In 1 Kings 3:24-25, the wise king said:

> *Bring me a sword; so they brought a sword for the king. He then gave an order; cut the living child in two and give half to one and half to the other. The woman whose son was alive was filled with compassion for her son and said to the king; please my lord, give her the living baby! Don't kill him. But the other said; neither I nor you shall have him. Cut him in two. Then the king gave his ruling: give the living baby to the first woman. Do not kill him; she is the mother. When all Israel heard the verdict the king had given, they held the king in awe, because they saw that he has wisdom from God to administer justice.*

Truly amazing! How many of us would have had that kind of wisdom to suggest such a thing as cutting the child in two? Solomon had wisdom from the Lord because the Lord came to him in a dream and said to Solomon, "Ask whatever you want me to give you," (1 Kings 3:5). Solomon made his request in 1 Kings 3:9-13:

> *So give your servant a discerning heart to govern your*

people and to distinguish between right and wrong; for who is able to govern this great people of yours. The Lord was pleased that Solomon had asked for this. So God said to him, since you have asked for this and not for long life or wealth for yourself, nor have asked for the death of your enemies but for discernment in administering justice. I will do what you have asked. I will give you a wise and discerning heart, so that there will not have been anyone like you, nor will there ever be. Moreover I will give you what you have not asked for – both riches and honor – so that in your lifetime you will have no equal among kings.

Like Solomon, we can ask the Lord for wisdom, as well, and He will give it to us. In James 1: 5-7, the Lord tells us:

If any of you lacks wisdom, he should ask God, who gives generously to all without finding fault, and it will be given to him. But when he asks, he must believe and not doubt, because he who doubts is like the wave of the sea, blown and tossed by the wind. That man should not think he will receive anything from the Lord; he is a double – minded man, unstable in all he does.

Yes, we can receive wisdom from the Lord; but it's up to us to apply that wisdom to all the areas of our lives. It's just like owning a Bible. How can it help you if you never open it and read it? Unlike most of us, Solomon had enough sense to recognize and acknowledge that it was wisdom that he needed most. He also knew that, once the Lord gave him wisdom, it was up to him to apply that wisdom to all the areas of his life. Somebody once said, "We must choose what the main thing is in our lives, then make sure that we keep the main thing the main thing. King David, King Solomon, Daniel, Apostle Paul, Hanna, Ruth, and Deborah, knew what the main thing was in their lives, and they kept the main thing the main thing. What is your main thing? Proverbs 1: 2-3 & 7 tells us that the book of Proverbs is for "attaining wisdom and discipline; for understanding words of insight; for acquiring a disciplined and prudent life, doing what is right, and just, and fair; and; the fear of the Lord is the beginning of knowledge, but fools despise wisdom and discipline." Attaining wisdom and a disciplined and prudent life -and doing what is right, just, and fair - are great aspirations to have as main things. Wouldn't you agree? Now, I'm not suggesting that your main thing should be the things mentioned here; but, if we could accomplish those few things, how much better would our lives be? How much more pleased would the Lord be with us? How much more could we accomplish in this life? How much more love, joy, peace, health, and prosperity of all kinds would we possess?

"It's up to us to apply the wisdom God gives us."

There's no telling what we could accomplish – the sky's the limit. I do believe the most important things in life are our relationships with the Lord and our family and close friends, then all the other success in life fall in as they may. That being said, the main thing should be our relationship and walk with the Lord; so, let's keep the main thing the main thing. The book of Proverbs has much to say about life – let's take a closer look, shall we? Proverbs 2:1-7 reads accordingly:

> *My son, if you accept my words and store up my commands within you, turning your ear to wisdom, and applying your*

heart to understanding, and if you call out for insight and cry aloud for understanding, and if you look for it as for silver and search for it as hidden treasure, then you will understand the fear of the Lord and find the knowledge of God. For the Lord gives wisdom and from his mouth come knowledge and understanding. He holds victory in store for the upright, he is a shield to those whose walk is blameless.

God can give us the gift of wisdom, but the scriptures tell us that we can search for it, as well. How do we do that? I have mentioned this several times and I will mention it here as well. I believe one of the best ways to search for wisdom is to bathe ourselves in all of scripture, but mainly Proverbs. As mentioned earlier, to bathe in scripture entails reading, meditating, and memorizing the Word. Pastor Jack recommended that I read the Bible out loud. His reasoning is, we are actually speaking the Word of God over our lives and hearing it as well. This is scriptural and there is power in speaking the Word over your life.

If we study Proverbs closely, we will find that this book gives us the primary guidelines to help us avoid the many pitfalls of life. We must realize that the Bible is God's primary way to reveal His wisdom for His children and all who read it. Yes, we will make mistakes in life - that's a given; but in Proverbs 2:10-11, the Lord tells us that "wisdom will enter your heart, and knowledge will be pleasant to your soul. Discretion will protect you, and understanding will guard you." Discretion is the ability to tell right from wrong, and how many of us could use a dose of that in our lives? I need several doses before I leave my home, and throughout the day, as well. Do I have this all worked out? Not hardly. It's a daily walk, but I must say this: When I stay plugged into my source, who is the Lord Jesus and His word, my decision-making and overall quality of life are much better, as opposed to not being plugged into the Lord and His word. Being plugged in is simply seeking God through reading His word and praying on a daily basis, then being obedient to the voice of the living God in Christ Jesus, who lives within us through the Holy Spirit.

Search for wisdom as you would a hidden treasure.

There were many times in my life when I thought I was making the right decision. The events that soon followed proved me wrong. I was disobedient in applying the wisdom that the Lord gave me. I knew the right thing to do, but I didn't do it. This brings us to other valid points about living and doing what we know to be right and true. As mentioned earlier, it's up to us to apply the wisdom that we have. This all comes down to obedience. Faith and obedience to the Lord in all our ways is the key that can unlock any door, remove any chains, and open up the voice of God in our hearts. Proverbs has been my favorite book in the Bible since I became a Christian in 1979. That's humbling to admit, because I have made some really stupid choices over the course of my Christian walk; and, with the guidance of Proverbs, one might wonder how that could happen. It always comes back to obedience and applying the Word, or the lack thereof. Some of my favorite scriptures are found in Proverbs. I would like to share them with you, here, if I may. Proverbs 3:5-8 says, "Trust in the Lord with all your heart and lean not on your own understanding; in all your ways submit to him, and he will make your paths straight. Do not be wise in your own eyes; fear the Lord and depart from evil, this will bring health to your body and nourishment to your bones.

Also, Proverbs 26:12 says, "Do you see a man wise in his own eyes? There is more hope for a fool than for him." People who are stuck in this rut are egomaniacs. This scripture makes you want to be very careful about your own assessment of yourself, doesn't it? The Bible also tells us, in Romans 12:3, "Do not think of yourself more highly than you ought, but rather think of yourself with sober judgment, in accordance with the measure of faith God has given you." There are many who underestimate themselves, while there are some who overestimate themselves. We should never make an evaluation of ourselves in accordance to how the world perceives us, but how God perceives us. What we accomplish here on earth is not our true worth, for we are worth more to the Lord than our mere earthly success, and it's the wisdom from the Lord that reveals this to us.

Do not be wise in your own eyes, fear the Lord and depart from evil

There are also many moral benefits to be received when applying wisdom. In Proverbs 2:16, Solomon says, "It [wisdom] will save you from the adulteress, from the wayward wife with her seductive words." (This scripture applies to both sexes) When people are tempted with this sin, God's power is their best defense, and – by far – their only defense. We always must remember who we are and whose we are. We are children of the Most High God. If ever tempted with this or any other sin, for that matter we should call upon the Lord and be transparent with him. We should do this not because he doesn't already know everything about us and the situation at-hand, but simply because when we call upon Him with total transparency, we are coming to Him with total trust and dependence and asking Him to join us in fighting off these and other temptations.

Apart from Christ, we can do nothing.

When we ask the Lord to join us, we are, in essence, telling Him that we can't get through this situation without Him: "I need you to walk through this with me, Lord, I can't do this on my own, please join me." That's what the Lord wants. Do you see it? The Lord always wants us to lean upon Him and share with Him how weak we are in these finite vessels of ours, and in every area of our lives. If we get to the point where we are self-sufficient apart from the Lord, we are headed for disaster. The Lord says, in John 15:5, "I am the vine; you are the branches. If a man remains in me and I in him, he will bear much fruit; apart from me you can do nothing." The kind of fruit the Lord is talking about in this passage is mentioned in Galatians 5:22, which says, "But the fruit of the Spirit is love, joy, peace, patience, kindness, goodness, faithfulness, and self-control. These fruits are the work of the Holy Spirit and can't be achieved in their fullness apart from Him. Many of us have failed miserably at attempting to receive these fruits apart from Christ. It's just not possible!

Another area where wisdom is crucial is the area of giving. During the early years of my Christian life, I must admit that tithing was difficult for me. I believe that's the way it is for most new Christians, and some seasoned ones, as well. Giving to the Lord is now a joy, and I can't imagine not doing so. The Lord revealed the truth to me about giving several years ago. Even then, though, I was reluctant to give. Why? In my opinion it all comes down to trusting that the Lord will do what he promises He will do. We also must know that everything we have belongs to the Lord, and He's watching us to see if we have been good stewards or not. The Lord tells us, in Proverbs 3:9-10, "Honor the Lord with your wealth and with the first fruits of your crops; then, your barns will be filled to overflowing and your vats will brim over with new wine. Notice that a promise follows after the command. Some of you may be thrown by the word *command*, but you must know that God doesn't make suggestions. He clearly states what He wants us to do. The Lord is not fickle; He knows exactly what He desires of us. The Lord gives commands because He is the almighty God, the everlasting Father, and the prince of peace. When He tells us what to do and we know it's of Him, we need to obey Him out of love, respect, and honor for him and have the faith and trust to know that the Lord always knows what's best for us.

Wisdom and understanding are of vital importance, especially for the Christian who desires to walk closely with the Lord and live the abundant life that he desires us to live. It is so important that Solomon says it this way, in Proverbs 4:6-7: "Do not forsake wisdom, and she will protect you; love her and she will watch over you. Though it cost all you have, get understanding." Though it cost all you have? That's a strong statement! If the Lord thinks wisdom and understanding are that important, shouldn't seeking out wisdom and understanding be a few of the things on our priority list? This is not a one-time search, like saying "I found it; now, I'm done." Seeking wisdom and understanding is a lifelong process and a moment-by-moment, day-by-day search. Why? I view it as a process because every day we are faced with new choices, and those choices always have consequences that go with them. The choices are typically good or evil, or somewhere in between; and, if it's somewhere in-between, it's definitely not good. This is the enemy's way of sugar-coating evil and wickedness. The Lord put it in Solomon's heart to know how important wisdom and understanding are.

Wisdom will protect you and watch over you.

As children of God, we need to heed this advice, because - without true wisdom and understanding from the Lord - the pitfalls of life could be many; and governing one's life and family are much too important to go without wisdom and understanding. Read Chapter 1:2 of Proverbs. This scripture will tell you what the book of Proverbs is for. I would share it with you, again, but I want you to open your Bible and see it there for yourself. Wisdom and understanding are so vital, Proverbs 16:16 says, "How much better to get wisdom than gold, to choose understanding rather than silver." I can't count the times I have heard people say that God doesn't know every move of every person on earth. How preposterous is that! The Lord tells us, in Proverbs 5:21, "For a man's ways are in full view of the Lord, and he examines all his paths. I have known of this scripture for many years and yet found myself in opposition to the Lord's will. I'm sure that many of my readers have known and read this same scripture, and yet found themselves in compromising situations. As believers, we don't even have to be aware that Proverbs 5:21 exists to realize that the Lord's eyes are everywhere, because we already know that He is omnipresent through the Holy Spirit. With that being said, it's really something different when we actually read it from the scriptures, instead of just saying that we know it. How many other things do we know of that aren't good for us and have participated in them anyway? The Lord must really want us to know He's aware of our every move, because Solomon mentions it again in Proverbs 15:3: "The eyes of the Lord are everywhere, keeping watch on the wicked and the good." Enough said, right? Not hardly. We're going to go even deeper. Why is it that, even though we know the Lord is watching us and is very aware of everything that we're doing - we keep on living, acting, and talking the same way? Why do we say in our hearts and minds, "I know I shouldn't do this, and I know that the Lord is watching me," and then go right on ahead with our plans? Doesn't that sound really stupid? It sounds stupid because it is stupid. I believe I have mentioned this next observation in another chapter, and it's worth repeating here. I have come to the conclusion that we willfully sin because we don't get disciplined for it immediately. The Lord says, in Romans 6:23; "For the wages of sin is death, but the gift of God is eternal life in Christ Jesus our Lord. If those wages were due immediately, how many of us would do that certain thing of which the Lord disapproves? The answer is, "Not many, if any at all." The Lord - in his wisdom, however - gave us our own will because He wants us to desire within ourselves to be obedient out of love, respect, and honor for Him, instead of obeying to escape discipline. Yes, even our obedience must be done with the right intentions.

The eyes of the Lord are always upon you.
He is always aware of your activities,
thoughts and motives.

Obedience comes with a price, and so does instruction. Proverbs 13:13 says, "He who scorns instruction will pay for it, but he who respects a command is rewarded." The Bible is our instruction book for every area of our lives; and, as mentioned in an earlier chapter, it will be repeated here, again, because it's one of the main things I want to get across in this book. Who knows more about life and the best way to live life than the one who created life? No one! As children of God, it's not in our best interest to scorn the instruction from the word of God because, just as the scripture says, we will pay for it; but if we heed the instruction in the Word, then the Lord will reward us. If we truly want to hear from God, we must not ignore the word of God. The best way to hear from God is to bathe ourselves in the word of God and prayer, along with obedience, then be still and listen for that gentle and quiet voice of the Lord through the Holy Spirit.

The Lord also tells us to be mindful of those with whom we keep company. Proverbs 13:20 says, "He who walks with the wise grows wise, but a companion of fools suffers harm." This is not to say that we shouldn't have friends who aren't saved and walking with the Lord, but I believe one of the things Solomon is warning us about is to be careful and guard against being influenced by others whose beliefs differ from our Christian beliefs, which are based on Biblical values. In other words, people who aren't acquainted with the Lord's ways aren't concerned with Biblical values in the same way as we who are sold out on Christ and the Word of God; therefore, having no concern for Biblical values, their worldly views and values will always surface in conversation.

Never compromise your beliefs to please or fit in with anyone.

My youngest daughter, Brittany, says it best when she says, "Daddy, just cover yourself in prayer and with the word of God, and the Lord will guard your heart when you're in the presence of worldly people, and He will protect your heart and mind from anything they may say or do. Now, that's what I call a wise young woman. The Holy Spirit has taught her very well. As Christians, we need not dodge the people who believe differently than we do; but, when we're around them, let's be careful not to talk and act like they do. Be careful, instead, to talk and act like our belief system entails, which is based on the word of God. We must never compromise our belief system to make someone else happy or to fit in with them. With that being said, let's not lose touch with the people whom we admire. I'm talking about the people who have great relationships with their family and children, their spouse or girlfriend, their faith and walk with the Lord Jesus Christ, and their overall life. I'm talking about individuals who have walked with the Lord and have set good examples for their children and for everyone who comes into their presence.

Granted, no one is perfect, and we all have our stuff that we're dealing with; however, I'm sure you know exactly what I'm talking about. We need to be spending quality time and/or staying in touch with the people whom we admire. In all reality, they are helping us become the person that the Lord wants us to become. In contrast, the man who is not influenced by Biblical values will typically not be the person to directly help you achieve your God-given purpose. The man who truly loves the Lord and is sold out on the word of God - knowing that the Bible is God's love letter to all humanity and truly desires to obey the Lord in all things - is the wise man about whom the scripture is talking when it says, "He who walks with the wise grows wise." This makes so much sense and is really simple to apply to life.

Guard your mind and your heart when you're around people of different belief systems.

Throughout our lives, we make plans to do certain things; and our ways always seem to be ok in our eyes. It's obvious that Solomon made some wrong choices in his day, because the Lord impressed upon his heart these very things. Proverbs 16:1-3 says, "To man belongs the plans of the heart, but from the Lord comes the reply of the tongue. All a man's ways seem innocent to him, but motives are weighed by the Lord. Commit to the Lord whatever you do, and your plans will succeed." Notice, in verse one, we have to answer to the Lord when our hearts are set on certain plans, and the results of our plans are always in His hands. This is not saying that we shouldn't plan; but, when we plan, we should plan with the Lord's will in mind. We, as Christians, never should make life's plans without consulting the Lord. When we consult with the Lord through prayer, praise, and worship, we are actually giving God Lordship over our plans. This is a must for the Christian who wants to put the Lord first in his or her life. As I have said in an earlier chapter, I have moved ahead of God's time-table more times than I care to say; and the plans that I made never worked out for any long-term success in any endeavor. Proverbs 16:2 tells us that we have a way of always justifying our ways, but the Lord is always aware of our true motives. It's time to take an inventory of our true motives. The Lord also tells us, in Proverbs 27:17, "As Iron sharpens iron, so one man sharpens another." There was a time in my life when I thought I had it all together, and getting another man's viewpoint was out of the question. I know there are people who are stuck in the same rut that I was in, and they are too proud to go get counseling or to listen to a friend who can clearly see some things that need some attention in their lives. We discussed pride in another chapter, so we won't be discussing it here; however, I do want to point out that it is pride that prevents man from seeking, listening, and applying nuggets of truth from his Christian brothers. This pride definitely will prevent anyone from moving closer to God's intended purpose for their lives. I have been through many a pit-fall in my day, and I believe most of them could have been prevented if I had listened to a few of my Christian brothers in Christ and - at other times - sought out my Christian brothers, and most of all being obedient to the Word of God.

"Iron sharpens iron. . . . Don't be too proud to listen to a Christian brother in Christ."

The Lord put Proverbs 27:17 in the Bible for a reason; and the reason is because God never intended for man to go it alone in tough times. If you don't have a Christian brother or sister in Christ whom you can bounce things off of, I highly recommend that you find one. Many times, the Lord will speak to you through other people; and, when you refuse to listen to a Christian brother in Christ, you are essentially refusing to listen to the Lord. At least listen, pray, and then go see what the scriptures say about what they said.

Proverbs 12:1 says, "Whoever loves discipline loves knowledge, but he who hates correction is stupid." The person who is too prideful to listen to constructive criticism is the person who hasn't learned much in life and will continue to be unlearned.

The Bible calls them stupid because they don't want to listen to correction. As a real estate appraiser, I have to sit in 14 hours of continuing education classes every year to renew my license. I can sit there brain-dead if I choose to, and not learn a thing; however, if I want to learn, I must submit myself to the teaching. My point is that for a person to learn from correction, they must open their ears, mind, and heart, as well. If that person does not willfully listen and open his or her mind and heart to what's being taught or spoken, no knowledge or truth will ever be learned. The same applies in life. One must be open in mind and spirit to receive from the Lord, or whatever the source, then have the obedience to apply the lesson. We must learn – and the sooner, the better - that continued mistakes and a lifestyle of disobedience can and will change the direction of our lives. The Lord's purpose in our lives remains the same, but the repercussions of mistake after mistake and willful disobedience positions us further from the Lord's intended purpose for our lives. I have learned the hard way most of my life, and my desire is that the words printed in this book - and especially in this chapter - will help you understand just how important it is to consult with the Lord and include Him in every area of your life. This point brings us to Proverbs 16:3, which says, "Commit to the Lord whatever you do, and your plans will succeed." This scripture teaches us to commit, submit, give, pray, praise, and worship our way through everything. When we commit to the Lord in whatever we do, like the scripture says, we give it to the Lord in prayer and trust Him to walk through whatever it is with us. We must never go it alone, without the Lord. The commentary in the Life Application Bible says this: "We must maintain a delicate balance, trusting God as if everything depended upon Him, while working as if everything depended upon us." That's a great statement, and I've heard several other speakers and authors say the same thing. It's so true and practical, and it is some of the best advice that people ever could apply to their lives. There have been many times during my lifetime when I did not understand the meaning of certain events that occurred in my life, let alone understanding why they occurred. There were many circumstances in my life that were created because of my unwise decisions; then, there were things that came about, which I had no idea why they happened. There are many circumstances that touch the lives of all people, as well as tragic events that happen in our country and around the world. We may, one day, have the answers to some things and yet never even come close to understanding the whys of other things. Solomon was a very astute and wise man; and, as evidenced by Proverbs 20:24, he has experienced some events in his life that even he did not understand. Proverbs 20:24 says, "A man's steps are directed by the Lord, how then can anyone understand his own way? The Lord is telling us to not worry about past events and the events in our lives that we don't understand. The Lord is basically telling us not to be concerned about the things that we don't understand, but trust Him in all things.

We don't need to understand everything, but we do need to trust God in everything.

He wants us to completely put our trust in Him. He wants us to know that he knows everything about what's going on in our lives and around the world, and that He has His own reasons for letting certain events come about. He also wants us to know that His timing is always perfect, even though we may not understand it. An appropriate scripture for this study is found in Isaiah 55:8-9, which says, "For my thoughts are not your thoughts, neither are your ways my ways, declares the Lord. As the heavens are higher than the earth; so are my ways higher than your ways and my thoughts than your thoughts." I must confess that I have questioned God myself, and have asked that all-consuming question: Why? As believers, having faith in Christ and the word of God, and being aware of the above scriptures in Isaiah 55:8-9, I sometimes wonder how we question the events that come into our lives and the happenings around the world. God is all-powerful and can create, prevent, or let anything happen at any time that He so chooses to happen in our lives and around the world, without having to answer to anyone.

The next and last topic of this chapter is a touchy one, and in my opinion the principal can apply to both men and women. The Lord tells us in Proverbs 31:3 - "Do not spend your strength on women, your vigor on those who ruin kings." Notice that the scripture says, *women* and not *woman*. This passage does not condemn women, but it does condemn men who think they need to have more than one woman at a time. It's no secret that Solomon had many wives. The Bible tells us, in 1 Kings 11:3, "He had seven hundred wives of royal birth and three hundred concubines, and his wives led him astray." In my opinion, having seven hundred wives is just lunacy in any era or culture. Yes, Solomon's weakness apparently was women. Back in Solomon's day, it was typical for a man to have multiple wives – but seven hundred? I want to emphasize, here, that one partner (not same sex) for life is always our best choice; and if - for some reason - you end up single or divorced, just one partner at a time when dating is your best choice, as well. I do want to point out that my text "not same sex" referring to one partner, should not surprise any reader that is not a Christian because this book is written with Biblical values and should not be a surprise or view it as being judgmental. That's not my intention. We men can be very vulnerable when it comes to women. It seems that most men are likely to compromise what's in their best interest for the woman they most desire. I'm not quite sure about women because I'm a man, but I do believe that most Christian women are more loyal than most Christian men. Sorry guys, that's just the way I see it. Sometimes men may want to please women because of various reasons - mainly for their beauty and other more personal reasons. Then, many times, men have this desire because of our own weakness in the area of being insecure. Throughout my life, I have known many men who never have been alone – without a woman – for any length of time in their lives, while also having a woman "in the wings," so to speak, as they're trying to figure out a way to leave/break up with their present girlfriend.

**"Men and Women of God, don't compromise
your beliefs and convictions for
the Lord to be in any relationship."**

This is exactly what happened to Solomon. If you read 1 Kings 11:4-8, you will see that Solomon compromised his beliefs to please his wives. Again, I'm purposefully not posting the scripture here so you can open your Bible and read it for yourself. They led him astray in terms of following other gods. He followed Ashtoreth, the goddess of the Sidonians; and Molech, the detestable god of the Ammonites. The Bible says that Solomon did evil in the eyes of the Lord and he did not follow the Lord completely. The key word, here, is "completely." Partial obedience is still disobedience. Solomon did not completely turn away from the Lord, but what he did was a very serious matter. Solomon broke one of the most important commandments – to worship the Lord thy God only. He did this for the sake of pleasing his women. I must make a disclaimer, here, by saying that my intention is not, in any way, to discredit women or to put them down in any form. Solomon married heathen women who did not know the Lord God. He and his wives were unequally yoked. Solomon was totally at fault, here, for marrying women who practiced idolatrous worship. I think Solomon made a grave mistake of marrying too many women, as well. Sometimes, we have problems getting along with one person, let alone seven hundred. I think the main message, here, is not to mix different types of worship and religion when marrying or dating, because one of the two involved may be required to compromise his or her beliefs in some form or fashion; and that can lead to disaster and breed havoc in the relationship. I must say that it's a good idea not even to date outside of your religion in terms of the Biblical values that are so dear to us about Christ. The specific values of which I speak are the importance of the cross, and the shed blood of Christ as the remission for our sins, Christ being the only way to receive salvation, and Christ being our mediator – the one who pleads our case to our Heavenly Father.

As mentioned in an earlier chapter, trying to change other people only irritates us and ticks them off. This will never work!

Final Thoughts

Unfortunately, Solomon and his wisdom are unequaled today and never will be equaled. Although we may never attain the wisdom with which Solomon was gifted, let's not let that prevent us from seeking that kind of wisdom from the Lord. As we can see from the Proverbs of Solomon, wisdom is a very important thing to possess and, as it seems, we can't honestly run our lives and makes decisions for our families with the best possible outcomes without this wisdom. Some things to ponder: Have you made decisions in the past with less than desirable outcomes? Knowing what you know now, what would you have done differently? Yes, this is hindsight, but true wisdom from the Lord would give us sight at the beginning, or before a decision is made. Do you get it? Do you ask the Lord for wisdom daily? Could this possibly be the reason we don't have the Solomon kind of wisdom? Do we really want the kind of wisdom that Solomon had? There are some valid reasons as to why we don't have great wisdom. Have you ever really searched the reasons as to why you don't have true wisdom? Is having wisdom important to you? If it is, have you been searching for it as you would for lost treasure, like the Lord tells us to do? Yes, the Lord can give us wisdom, but have you really been searching for it? The Lord says if it costs all you have, get understanding. Do you want understanding this much? Are you wise in your own eyes? Do you think that you are above counseling? Are you not inclined to listen to other believers, even if you think you are more spiritual than they? Yes these are tough questions, but I really want you to dig down deep and think about these things. I really don't want to sugar-coat the principals of God for you just so you can feel warm and fuzzy all over.

I'm hoping that the words, sentences, and paragraphs, contained in this book will cause you to take a closer look at your life, your choices, and your actions, instead of looking at what's wrong with other people. It's not other people who are wrong with the world; – it's us, as individuals. We can't change other people, but we can change ourselves; and, by changing ourselves, we can impact everyone around us. Is it on your mind that the Lord is always aware of your thoughts, motives, and actions? I sincerely believe that if we would actively be aware of the Lord and his infinite knowledge, we would choose to live differently; this is where some of that wisdom may possibly stem from. Have you thought of the company that you're keeping lately? If your company is not of the same belief system as yours, do they have a positive effect on you, and are you having a positive effect on them? Always make sure you guard your heart when around non-believers, be in an attitude of prayer, and remember to practice your beliefs. We don't need to understand everything that the Lord allows and why He allows it, but we do need to trust Him in everything. Don't compromise your beliefs - under any circumstances - with anyone especially just to be in a relationship with someone who opposes your Christian beliefs. It doesn't matter how sweet or attractive the person may be. If his or her spiritual/ Christian beliefs are too far apart from yours for comfort, and if you think you can change or fix that person, then disaster is brewing. That will not work!

Chapter Ten

Running the Race

What's your life's mission? Are you making a statement with your life? Of course you are, but what kind of statement are you making? Are you making a statement for the Lord or for the world? Are you in the race? If so, what race are you in? Where are you in the race? Are you running the race with everything you've got, or are you just getting by? Are you running the race like you want to win? Have you ever been in a race that you regret even being in? Are you presently in a race that you wish you were not? Have you been distracted by someone or something during the race? We will discuss some of these questions, while believing that the Lord will reveal to you some of the things that have been holding you back in running heaven's race. If you haven't trusted Jesus Christ as your personal savior, you're not even in the most important race of all.

What is the most important race? In Philippians 3:14, the Apostle Paul says, "I press on toward the goal to win the prize for which God has called me heavenward in Christ Jesus." Also, 1 Corinthians 9:24-27 says, "Do you not know that in a race all the runners run, but only one gets the prize. Run in such a way to get the prize. Everyone who competes in the games goes into strict training. They do it to get a crown that will not last; but we do it to get a crown that will last forever. Therefore I do not run like a man running aimlessly; I do not fight like a man beating the air. No, I beat my body and make it my slave so that after I have preached to others, I myself will not be disqualified for the prize." Yes this is the most important race of them all: the race to receive the crown of life when we leave this life and meet Jesus Christ. I'm a big golf and NASCAR fan; and, most Sunday's - if I'm home - you can catch me switching the channels from golf to NASCAR. In NASCAR, drivers must qualify for a starting position. Depending on the fastest qualifying run by the driver, they're placed in line according to their speed. In golf, typically before a player can get his PGA touring card, he must get through Q (qualifying) school. During a PGA tournament, once a player qualifies to be on the tour, he has two days to qualify, which is typically Thursday and Friday. After the day's end on Thursday, the PGA determines a cut-off point in terms of score. If a player's score doesn't meet the cut-off point, he or she does not qualify to play in the tournament on Saturday and Sunday. In golf terms, this is called making the cut. What does this have to do with the race for our heaven's crowns? Just as one must qualify to get a position in a NASCAR race - and play two rounds of golf in a PGA tournament to qualify to play on Saturday and Sunday - similarly, we must qualify to run for heaven's crowns. So, how do we qualify to run the race for the crown that Apostle Paul talks about? To be qualified to run heaven's race, one must be born-again. You may be familiar with the scripture in John 3:3, where Jesus says, "I tell you the truth, no one can see the kingdom of God unless he is born again." The invitation to run the race for heaven's crowns is open to everyone, but you can't run that race until you've accepted the Lord Jesus Christ as your personal Savior. When you accept the Lord as your personal Savior, you are then qualified to run the race for crowns to be received in heaven, because you are now born-again and have become a child of God. Accepting the Lord as your personal savior is of the utmost importance, because if you're not in the race for heaven's crowns, you are, nevertheless, running a race of some kind; and I assure you that the alternative race is not the race to be in. The crowns I'm talking about are the crowns that the Lord has reserved for his children when we meet Him face-to-face and he says, "Well done, my good and faithful servant."

The qualifications to run heaven's race do not depend on anything but your willingness to lay down your pride in a way that says, "Lord, I cannot and do not want to live life without you." Please forgive me for my sins, and have mercy on me. I accept you as my personal Savior, and I trust you to save me from my sins.

This is not a concrete prayer, but a guideline prayer to receive salvation. When you pray this prayer with all sincerity, you have just become a child of God; and, from that point on, you are indwelt with the Holy Spirit. You are now in the race for heaven's crowns. The best part about this race is that everyone who runs the race gets a crown. We are not running against each other, but are in a race with ourselves. Another great part is that we are not limited to one crown. There are multiple crowns available to us, so let's run the race, with everything we've got and get all the crowns we can. I believe that the Bible talks about five crowns - "the rewards in heaven" - and I won't go into detail what their meanings are, but I'd like to share them with you, here. Please note that different versions of the Bible may use different words to describe the crowns, and I think it's a great idea to set up study time and research, for yourself, what the reward of each crown is. The first crown is found in 1 Corinthians 9:25, which talks about an incorruptible crown. The second crown is found in 1 Thessalonians 2:19-20, which talks about a crown of rejoicing. The third crown is found in 2 Timothy 4:7-8, which talks about the crown of righteousness. The fourth crown is found in 1 Peter 5:2-4, which talks about the crown of glory; and the fifth crown is found in Revelation 2:10, which talks about the crown of life. The Bible also tells us, in Matthew 6:20, "But store up for yourselves treasures in heaven, where moths and vermin do not destroy, and where thieves do not break in and steal". So, along with crowns to be received, it's obvious – according to the scripture in Matthew, stated above - that there are other rewards to be received, as well. So, how do we store up treasures in heaven? Just a few examples are giving tithes and offerings, helping and showing love for the less fortunate, forgiving and showing compassion for others, and giving your time. The list is endless, and I think you get the idea.

Let's be careful to think that all we need to do is become saved, and nothing more. Many of us who are in the race act like it's not important to run with everything we've got. Why is it that most men wouldn't go to church if it wasn't for their wives making them go? Why is it that many of us don't think it's important to go to church? If the Lord didn't think church was important, He wouldn't have created the church. One of the Church's primary purposes is to teach us the word of God, help us understand how it applies to our everyday lives, and develop Christian fellowship. As Christians, we need to study the word of God so we can learn more about Jesus, his ways, and what he expects of us. Then, as we study the Lord's word, He not only enlightens us about himself, but He also reveals the parts of us that need to be changed and/or done away with. Once we make the decision to be obedient in ridding ourselves of the distasteful things that keep us down, the purifying process begins to take shape in our lives. Please don't let this point slip by you, because it can and will change your life as you know it.

As the Lord tells us, in Hebrews 10:25, "Let us not give up meeting together as some are in the habit of doing, but let us encourage one another, and all the more as you see the day approaching." Look here, children of God: We need spiritual guidance and fellowship to help us be all that God wants us to be and to be able to handle all that he wants to give us. If you think you're so spiritual and mature that you don't need mature Christian fellowship, then you've been blinded by the enemy and he has you right where he wants you: full of pride and self. In an earlier chapter, we discussed being self-righteous and how pride comes before the fall. Also, if you're one who has been neglecting your Church services and a Sunday School or group, and you've been a Christian for quite some time, it's obvious there's something that's hindering you; and, for your own good and the good of yourself and family, you should put it on your priority list to find out just what exactly that hindrance is. It's very difficult for Christians to run the race that the Lord has ordained for them to run if they have a constant hindrance or hindrances in their life. Why? First of all, when the Lord says to throw off all that hinders there surely must be a good reason for it. A hindrance is basically a factor causing trouble in achieving a positive result, or tending to produce a negative result. Merriam Webster translates hindrance as "something that stands in the way of one's progress or achievement"

Wow! Having a hindrance doesn't sound like it's a good thing to have, now, does it? No wonder the Lord tells us to throw off all that hinders. How many of us want trouble to rear its head when we're looking for a positive result and, instead, a negative result occurs? How many of us want something to stand in the way of our achievement or progress? I'm sure there is no one in his or her right mind who wants negative results and/or opposition in any form to stand in their way of achievement or progress. Then, why do we keep hanging on to our hindrances, as if they're our prize possessions? Yes, I'm talking about me too. In fact, everything I talk about in this book is something I have dealt with and/or experienced in some form or fashion. I share this with you to give you some kind of comfort in knowing that it's not just you - but me, too, as well as the people you work with, the guy at the grocery store, your fellow church members, and - yes - even your spouse or the person you are dating. No one is perfect. Everyone has hindrances, but not everyone is willing to be honest with themselves, and do what's necessary to be healed of them. If you're anything like I was, you are not going to want to be found out. Let's find out what's hindering us and deal with it in the proper way. Then, let's get on with running this race, and do it God's way.

In Hebrews 12:1, the Apostle Paul tells us how to run the race: "Therefore, since we are surrounded by a great cloud of witnesses, let us throw off everything that hinders and the sin that so easily entangles. And let us run with perseverance the race marked out for us, fixing our eyes on Jesus, the pioneer and perfecter of faith. We have so many things working against us today, in the form of distractions and hindrances, that sometimes it's difficult to centralize our focus on the more important things. This is why Paul tells us to fix our eyes on Jesus. How do we fix our eyes on Jesus? You have read this several times throughout this book, and you will read it again here. The best way I know to do this is to bathe ourselves in the word of God and in prayer, and to praise and worship him. Also,

I might add we should do these things not just on Sunday, but every day of the week. Another way to fix our eyes on Jesus is to memorize the words of Christ and meditate on them. If we're just attending Church services - and that's it - we're seriously missing the mark, big time. Also, if you're not one to attend Church, and you say that you're a believer, then it's time to take a serious look at the reason you're not attending Church, because there's a great possibility that Satan is hindering you in some way, and you need to get to the bottom of it immediately.

Have you set special quiet time aside in the morning with the Word and prayer, or are you having that time with the Lord on the fly while you're driving to work? If the former is the case, keep it up; this is a good thing. Spending time on the fly, however, should be done in addition to setting some special time aside to pray and fellowship with the Lord before your day begins. This was mentioned before in another chapter and is worth repeating because it's vital in your personal relationship with the Lord. I know there are many who say, "I just don't have the time. I barely leave for work on time." How about getting up a little earlier – let's say fifteen to twenty minutes earlier? Try spending some quality time with the Lord, and then continue on your fellowship with Him as you're driving to work. There may be many of you who aren't having that quiet time in the morning; and you're not even having it in your car as you're driving to work, because you're in the habit of jamming out to your secular tunes in the morning, or thinking about your workday. I know because I used to do it, myself. I like music as much as anyone; and, yes, some secular music as well. In my personal opinion, though, it would do all of us much good to shut off the racket in the morning and spend that time with the Lord. Even if it's just saying the words, "Speak to me Lord," then being silent and waiting to hear from Him.

I confess that I used to be like most people: As soon as I got in my car, I'd turn on the radio or put a Rock CD in and rock on. Yes, praise and worship music are great in the mornings, as well, and have their place in spending time with the Lord, but nothing can replace that quiet time with the Lord, which is one of the most overlooked and important ingredients when it comes to fixing our eyes on Jesus. One of the most important aspects of fixing our eyes on Jesus is listening to his ever so soft voice through his spirit that dwells inside us; and this just can't be done with all the racket of music, no matter how spiritual it is. Sometimes you just have to be quite.

Another aspect of this race we're in is the all important ingredient of focusing on our goal. Watching the best in the world at anything is truly amazing. It's mind-boggling to hear some of the Olympic athletes' stories of the kinds of training they participated in and how hard they had to train in order to excel in their events. It's vital for them to have focus in their personal lives, as well as in their training. Just as it's important for an athlete to have focus in their personal and training lives, it's equally important for us to have that similar kind of focus in our personal and spiritual lives when running the race for heaven's crowns. Training for heaven's crowns is, by far, the most important training that you will ever be faced with in your lifetime. As mentioned before, everybody who's qualified to run in heaven's race wins and receives a crown, but let's not run casually. Let's run the race as if it's the Olympics, where there is only one winner.

As mentioned earlier, the Lord tells us to run, with perseverance, the race marked for us. Just before He tells us to run with perseverance, he tells us to throw off everything that hinders and the sin that so easily tangles. Why did the Lord tell us first to throw off everything that hinders? He tells us this because the things that distract us hinder us from running our best race. Some of the things that hinder us may be sin, and some may not be sin; nevertheless, they hinder and are a distraction. It's up to each of us, individually, to be totally honest and transparent with ourselves and admit what hinders us from running our best race. Most of us know what hinders us. Many of the things that hinder us come in different forms, including marriage, stress, career, family, money, debt, dating relationships, friends, or the lack thereof - and the list goes on. Please know that I'm not saying these things are bad; but, many times, they bring stress in our lives; and stress that is not monitored and/or managed well can take a toll on every part of our lives. When we have hindrances, of any kind, we lose our focus; and that's exactly why the Lord tells us to throw them off. Many people have no focus, due to a lack of discipline and just living their lives by the seat of their paints. In other words, they do what they want, when they want, with whom they want, and with no regard, whatsoever, to what the Lord may think about what they are doing. The say, this is my life, and I can live it any way I choose. Basically, when anyone thinks like this, he or she is saying, I don't need God's help, and I can go it alone. They say as long as I'm not hurting anyone, it's ok - I know what I'm doing. Yes, I have been there, done that, and said those very same things when I was young and not so bright. This is not a good way to live, especially if you're a born again Christian, because you are in heaven's race.

As a single father, I do want to discuss my lessons learned from dating. I'm not going to go into much detail, because this is not a book about dating; there are, however, a few things that I would like to share with you that distracted and hindered me from running heaven's race. As mentioned in an earlier chapter, I'd like to use my dating experience as an example. I'm not sure if it was dating that I was doing, or just wasting time and money. Well, maybe it was a little of both. I would meet a woman once and never see her again. I don't consider that dating as much as just meeting and interviewing each other. Yes, I met a few nice women whom I dated for a few months, and I now consider them friends; but, for the most part, I was not actually dating anyone seriously, because I didn't get a green light from God to move ahead in the friendship. During this time of my life, I must say that I was being hindered by the whole dating process because it was taking most of my spare time in the evening and has managed to take hold of my thoughts during the day. Spending hours upon hours online, sending and answering emails, became another job. The problem was I let it consume me. During those few years of dating, I wrote four chapters of this book – not very good, is it?

When I threw off what hindered me "dating," I wrote the remaining six chapters in three months: You be the judge. This is just a good example of how much more effective we can be without hindrances in our lives. I take full responsibility for my choices and surely don't blame anyone I met. I'm very grateful to the Lord for revealing to me what was going on in this process. Finally, I let go of the trappings and hindrances of all the glitz and glamour of internet dating, as I knew it, and I'm sure that many of you single men and women can relate to what I'm talking about.

There are pros and cons to everything, including being single. If we who are single are not careful, our social lives can and will steal our dreams; and the important things in life will be left undone or – worse, yet – forgotten. We must be wise in how we manage our time and social activities. I'm going to be very blunt here, and this may be hard for some of you. I'm sure there are many single Christians who are in romantic relationships for all the wrong reasons; and I have been in my own, as well. It's time to be honest and start asking these questions: Am I dating this person for the right reasons? Is this the person I want to spend the rest of my life with? Is this the person with whom God has me spending the rest of my life with? Has this person helped me grow closer to the Lord? Will this person support me in my God given purpose? Does this person love the Lord, and does he/she have a personal relationship with Him? If your answer to any of these questions is no, then you are and have been distracted by this relationship; and, yes, it is a hindrance to you.

You most likely are familiar with the scripture in 2 Corinthians 6:14, which says, "Do not be yoked together with unbelievers." Yes, as most believe this scripture is directed toward Christians marrying people who are not Christians. I would like to point out that there are many other ways to be unequally yoked that can cause hindrances in a believer's life and that can and will prevent him or her from running their best race. I won't labor on this point, but I would like to touch on a just few things, like distracting personality differences, conflicting lifestyle interests, disturbing habits. I'm sure you get the idea. There are many things that can be distractions and/or hindrances in dating.

If you've been dating a person for multiple years and are still not sure that you want to spend the rest of your life with him or her, then that person is more than likely not the one for you. In fact, that person may be the very distraction and/or hindrance keeping you from running your best race for heaven's crowns, and keeping you from excelling in life. It took me fifty years to figure this out, and I surely hope it doesn't take you as long. If you stay plugged in to the Lord through praising God, worshiping Him, praying, reading and meditating on the Word, and having fellowship with other believers who are walking with the Lord, and being obedient to the Lord, chances of success in all areas of your life will be much greater. I am not saying that you won't have any problems or pitfalls; but, when you stay plugged in to the Word of God and godly Christian people, you may very well recognize the hindrances sooner, see them as they're trying to come into your life, and possibly deter them all together.

Many times in life, doing the right thing is one of the hardest things to do. Yes, there are many things that hinder us, but I wanted to touch on the subject of being single and dating, because I know from personal experience just how bad dating choices can hinder every endeavor in life, especially your personal relationship with the Lord. I'm not saying that dating is a bad thing; but, when dating, we must know when something hinders us, as well as when we are a hindrance to someone. We must listen to the Lord when he says to throw off everything that hinders. As mentioned earlier, the Lord doesn't make requests or suggestions. He gives commands because he is our Lord and God.

The Lord is always with you, and He's fully aware of the condition of your heart. I have learned to call upon Jesus in my time of need and loneliness, as well as when everything in life appears to be going my way. I've also learned that I never should make decisions based on my emotions, especially in times of loneliness and fear, just to be in a dating relationship that I know I shouldn't be in. All men and women should refrain from getting into a dating relationship until all of their emotional and mental scars have been healed; otherwise, the scars will hinder you more than you may realize. Hopefully, this chapter will prompt you to dig deeper within yourself, so you can become better acquainted with yourself and be totally transparent and honest with yourself, as well. C'mon now, most of you know some of the things that are holding you back and you just can't let go for whatever the reason. You can do this! With God all things are possible!

For those of you who don't have a clue as to what the hindrances are that are holding you back, I strongly suggest that you bring this issue of hindrances to the Lord and then seek out a good Christian counselor. One who is trained in identifying spiritual roots, such as a Prayer Deliverance Minister like my dear friend, Pastor Jack Valentino of Sword of the Spirit Healing Ministries. Let's be real and transparent here: More than likely, there are, presently, things which are hindering you in your life and preventing you from hearing some very important information that the Lord is trying to get to you concerning His will for your life. These are the hindrances that have kept you from running the race the way God has planned for you to do. Because of those hindrances, however, you have the Lord's hands tied, so to speak. We never will be able to run the race that the Lord has planned for us if we continually try to have it our way. I want to clarify, again, that your hindrance may or may not be sin; but if it is sin, then that's a definite road block to your running the race He has planned for you. Secondly, even if your hindrance isn't a sin, it's a hindrance, nevertheless; and the Lord tells us to throw off everything that hinders. Why? Well, He tells us to do this because, most of the time, it's the hindrances we have in our lives that keep us distracted from Him, His word, and His ever-so-soft voice that lives within us through the Holy Spirit. Those hindrances keep us preoccupied with the things that are holding us back from everything the Lord has for us. There is no such thing as standing still in life. Either we're moving forward or backward by our daily activities and obligations. When we hang on to our hindrances, we are definitely not moving forward, but farther away from God's intended purpose for our lives.

As mentioned earlier, many times, our hindrances come from our jobs, business dealings, family conflict, social connections, and the list goes on. Now, I'm not suggesting that you leave your business, job, family, or friends; but I am suggesting that you seriously take a look at your life with much transparency and ask the Lord to reveal the hindrances that are affecting your relationship with Him. I understand that things aren't always as easy as they appear on paper; but we all need to start somewhere, and a good place for all of us to start is to identify our hindrances, change our outlook on the thing or things that are hindering us, and work toward ridding ourselves of them. "throw them off." Most people go through life without ever taking inventory of the things that may be hindering them. It's never too late to start cleaning out the closet. Let's identify those hindrances, get rid of them, and run the race that the Lord has set before us. Much of the time, some simple changes may need to be made to get rid of some hindrances.

Now that we know we must run the race like we want to win and throw off all that hinders us, how do we do that? Earlier in this chapter, we discussed how hard and long the Olympic athletes trained in order to get in position to win. We must have similar drive, desire, and discipline as Olympians have when running heaven's race. We must want heaven's crowns that badly. As the saying goes, hindsight is twenty-twenty. For many years, I lived with the things that were hindering me, mainly because I had no idea what they were, let alone that they were hindrances. I used to think, "It's no big deal." I honestly had no idea that some of the things that I found out were hindrances in my life were shaping my life; and, in a way, that was keeping me from the Lord's intended purpose for my life. Yes, there were things that I knew were not in my best interest; but, for the most part, I had no idea how certain things, as well as people, could be hindrances and play a major role in shaping my life. Common sense says that if something hinders you, you should get rid of it.

Ok, married couples, if you think your spouse is hindering

you, don't think you need to get rid of him or her. The Lord is not referring to that. If that's the case, please go see a professional in the Christian arena and find out what the problems are, and fight for your family and marriage. The Bible tells us that Satan came to kill, steal, and destroy; and he will do just that if you let him. One of the ways he does this is by trying to keep you in your hindrances. Again, sometimes more often than not when we have hindrances, we lose our focus in life. Why? The reason is because our hindrances have us preoccupied. In an earlier chapter, we discussed wisdom and how there is more hope for a fool than for a man who is wise in his own eyes. That was me, in a nutshell. I thought I had it all together, and I never gave it a second thought of how relationships, social life, and habits could be a hindrance. I must mention this: When you choose to date someone who has not resolved his or her past hurts – someone who is holding on to un-forgiveness for anyone, you are, in essence, walking through a land mine of pain in that relationship, as well as creating a huge hindrance for yourself. Most single people have no business dating and getting into relationships until they have identified their past hindrances and, taken them to the Lord in prayer, and trust Him to heal them of whatever it is that requires healing in their lives. As I look back five, ten, twenty, and even thirty years ago, I can now see the things that were a hindrance to me, how they hindered and shaped my walk with the Lord, and how they affected my success both earlier and later in life. Thankfully, though, the Lord says that all things work together for the good to those who love Him. The enemy sure has a way of keeping us in his grip, and he does so by feeding us lies and trying to make us believe that we're on the right track – while, the whole time, we're actually on the wrong track and being hindered. In my lifetime, I have met many people who are being hindered by their lifestyle, beliefs, and social connections.

Granted, I don't claim to have all the answers; and I don't claim to understand every word of the Bible, but I do believe that I am on the right path – finally. What's the right path? If you've come this far in reading this book, you surely know what path I'm talking about. It's the path of the Lord Jesus Christ and everything that he teaches us in the Bible, which he left for us; this is the path. Obedience to the Lord is the key principal in following this path. Psalms 119:105 says, "For the word is a lamp unto my feet and a light unto my path."

Final Thoughts

Have you thought about the kind of statement that you're making with your life? Do you even care about the kind of statement that you're making? Are you concerned that the statement you're making with your life is impacting your loved ones and people all around you? Now that you're finishing this chapter, have you considered the things in your life, which may be hindering you from running heaven's race? If you're not sure what your life's purpose is, could there be a hindrance of some kind that is preventing you from knowing what that purpose is? If you're in the race, are you running it like you want to win, or are you in the race at a spectator's pace? If not, then what has you distracted? Are you even concerned that there are distractions in your life? Do you even know what race you're in? Are you in the most important race of all – heaven's race? Are you qualified to run heaven's race? You must be a born-again believer in the Lord Jesus Christ to be qualified to run heaven's race. Have you accepted Jesus as your personal savior? Are you one who neglects church or thinks that it's not important to go to church? Have you considered that it was Christ who created the church? If Christ didn't think the church was necessary, he wouldn't have created it. Are you training to run heavens race? Everyone on the planet has an invitation to run heaven's race. Have you accepted the invitation? Have you considered that there may be a hindrance from the enemy that is preventing you from totally giving yourself to the Lord? If so, are you ok with that? Do you remember that a hindrance is something that stands in the way of one's progress or achievement? Have you considered that the Lord really wants to bless you, but you have His hands tied because you choose to do things your way instead of His way? Have you had your eyes fixed on Christ, or have you at least been trying to learn how to fix your eyes on Him on a daily basis? Have you been spending quality time with the Lord?

Why I Wrote This Book

I wrote this book for many reasons, but there are three primary reasons why I wrote it. The first is, if you're not dead, and you're breathing – you're wounded, and you need to know it. The second reason is; you need to learn about your wounded-ness, and come to terms with why you act, think, behave, and believe the way you do. And the third reason is, the Holy Spirit commissioned me to write this book, so I could be of help in pointing the wounded spirit to Jesus, because there is no true and lasting healing apart from Him.

There are many false doctrines being taught about how to be with God when we leave our earthly bodies. Jesus says, I am the way the truth and the life, no one comes unto the Father except by me. I wanted to share the truth about what God's word says concerning that choice. Eternity is much too long to be wrong.

Have I arrived in my complete healing? Of course not, and neither will you until Christ returns to take us home. Yes, there are some wounds that the Lord may choose to heal instantaneously, then there are others that are moment by moment processes, and over a period of time, the healing becomes more apparent, and it's these that are my concern. I hope to share some nuggets of truths that will help deliver you from fear to faith - from hate to love - and from an un-forgiving spirit to a forgiving spirit – and much more.

Bio

When you need a friend, Robert Jones is available. He is a good listener and does not judge. He will console you and empathize with you but he won't enable you. He will remind you that Jesus loves you and will walk beside you, and if you turn your life over to Jesus great things will happen. Through this book he will be that friend to you, too.

Robert turned his life over to Jesus when he was twenty two years of age and has been cultivating that relationship ever since. He has been blessed in his personal and professional life. Robert makes his living as a commercial real estate appraiser and has three beautiful daughters and a handsome grandson.

Robert is a man of integrity and strongly believes that the seed principal is not biased in that, what a person sows he will surely reap. Robert's father was a man who has never met a stranger, and has passed that trait along to him. So, if you ever have the opportunity to meet Robert, please don't hesitate because he would be honored with your presence and would love to meet you.

Contact the author
Email: robert@thinklikegod.org
Website: ThinkLikeGod.org

Need Additional Copies?

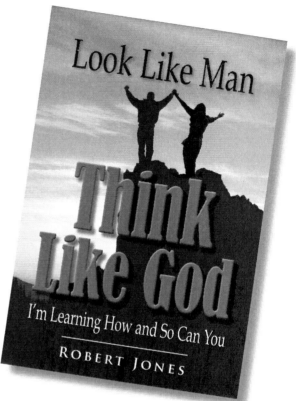

To order more copies of

Look Like Man
Think Like God

contact NewBookPublishing.com

❐   Order online at:
    NewBookPublishing.com/Bookstore

❐   Call 877-311-5100 or

❐   Email Info@NewBookPublishing.com

Reliance Media